SLEEPWALKING TO ARMAGEDDON

Also by Helen Caldicott

Crisis Without End: The Medical and Ecological Consequences of the Fukushima Nuclear Catastrophe

If You Love This Planet: A Plan to Save the Earth

War in Heaven: The Arms Race in Outer Space

*Loving This Planet:
Leading Thinkers Talk About How to Make a Better World*

Nuclear Power Is Not the Answer

*The New Nuclear Danger:
George W. Bush's Military-Industrial Complex*

Nuclear Madness

Missile Envy: The Arms Race and Nuclear War

SLEEPWALKING TO ARMAGEDDON

THE THREAT OF NUCLEAR ANNIHILATION

edited by
HELEN CALDICOTT

THE NEW PRESS

25 YEARS

NEW YORK
LONDON

Requests for permission to reproduce selections from this book should be mailed to: Permissions Department, The New Press, 120 Wall Street, 31st floor, New York, NY 10005.

Published in the United States by The New Press, New York, 2017
Distributed by Perseus Distribution

LIBRARY OF CONGRESS CATALOGING-IN-PUBLICATION DATA

Names: Caldicott, Helen, editor of compilation.
Title: Sleepwalking to Armageddon : the thread of nuclear annihilation / edited by Helen Caldicott.
Other titles: Threat of nuclear annihilation
Description: New York : The New Press, 2017 | Includes bibliographical references.
Identifiers: LCCN 2017004869 | ISBN 9781620972465 (hardcover : alk. paper)
Subjects: LCSH: Nuclear warfare. | Nuclear weapons. | Nuclear disarmament. | Nuclear warfare--Prevention. | World politics--21st century.
Classification: LCC U263 .S595 2017 | DDC 355.02/17--dc23 LC record available at https://lccn.loc.gov/2017004869

The New Press publishes books that promote and enrich public discussion and understanding of the issues vital to our democracy and to a more equitable world. These books are made possible by the enthusiasm of our readers; the support of a committed group of donors, large and small; the collaboration of our many partners in the independent media and the not-for-profit sector; booksellers, who often hand-sell New Press books; librarians; and above all by our authors.

www.thenewpress.com

This book was set in Janson Text and Berthold Akzidenz Grotesk
Jacket illustration by Malgorzata Bedowska

Printed in the United States of America

10 9 8 7 6 5 4 3 2 1

Contents

Introduction

Helen Caldicott

Despite Donald Trump's vows to seal the U.S. border and eradicate ISIS, the real terrorists of the world today are the United States and Russia. They possess 94 percent of the nuclear weapons on the planet, and they hold the rest of the world hostage to their provocative and self-serving foreign policies and misadventures. As a result, we are closer to nuclear war now, at the start of the twenty-first century, than we've ever been before, even during the height of the Cold War.

While we must be concerned about global warming—the other existential threat to the planet—it is imperative that we do not take our eyes off the nuclear threat. To do so is to risk sleepwalking to Armageddon. Nine countries around the globe are known to have nuclear weapons, many of them on hair-trigger alert. In at least five separate locations in the world, two or more nuclear-armed countries are in actual or proxy wars or standoffs that could escalate at any time. And the United States has elected to the presidency a man who seems to feel that, because they exist, nuclear weapons ought to be used. Donald Trump has implied that he feels tactical nuclear weapons can be effectively employed in battle and seemed to imply in comments about Japan, South Korea, and Saudi Arabia that he had few concerns about proliferation of nuclear weapons to additional countries.

Tony Schwartz, the co-writer of Trump's bestselling book

Trump: The Art of the Deal, who spent eighteen months "camping out in [Trump's] office, joining him on his helicopter, tagging along at meetings, and spending weekends with him at his Manhattan apartment and his Florida estate," listening in on Trump's business meetings and phone conversations, told Jane Mayer of the *New Yorker* that if he were titling Trump's book today, instead of *The Art of the Deal*, Schwartz would call it *The Sociopath*. Schwartz has tweeted, "Trump is totally willing to blow up the world to protect his fragile sense of self. Please God don't give this man the nuclear codes." And Mayer reports that Schwartz said, "I genuinely believe that if Trump wins and gets the nuclear codes there is an excellent possibility it will lead to the end of civilization."[1]

During the Cold War, there were restraints on either side between Russia and America. Now, for the first time since the Cold War ended, Russia and America are confronting each other militarily with seemingly no restraints. During the political debate preceding the 2016 American presidential election, Marc Rubio, Ted Cruz, Donald Trump, and Hillary Clinton were overtly discussing the notion of bombing such countries as Syria, Iran, Yemen, and others. And all of them have discussed the use of nuclear weapons.

To understand what drives America's frighteningly militaristic stance and warmongering, follow the money. After the Cold War ended, U.S. negotiators promised Mikhail Gorbachev that America would not enlarge NATO, and the world enjoyed a period of relative peace. But the United States reneged on its promise a few short years later: "No war" was bad for business! In 1997 Norman Augustine, the head of Lockheed Martin, traveled to Romania, Hungary, Poland, Czechoslovakia, and the other newly liberated Eastern European countries and asked: Do you want to join NATO and be a democracy? (Joining NATO doesn't make you a democracy.) But in order to join NATO, these small countries had to spend billions of dollars to buy weapons.[2]

That's the dynamic that instigated NATO's expansion from the end of the Cold War to the present time—right up to the border of Russia. Imagine if Russia expanded its territory to the border of Canada with the United States. Remember what America did when Russia placed nuclear weapons in Cuba? We were minutes from nuclear war. More recently, Hillary Clinton has been a recipient of huge amounts of money from the military-industrial complex. So are most members of the U.S. Congress and Senate, with the top donors including Lockheed Martin, Boeing, BAE Systems, Raytheon, Northrop Grumman, General Dynamics, and Airbus in Western Europe. America now wants to enlarge NATO forces and equipment to the tune of $3.4 billion. America also plans to spend $1 trillion over the next thirty years, replacing every single hydrogen bomb, submarine, ship missile, and airplane. In order for Barack Obama to persuade the U.S. Senate to ratify the START III treaty in 2010, he had to promise Senator Jon Kyl (R-AZ), a leading conservative on military issues, that he would replace every single nuclear weapon and delivery system. In the context of these provocations, Vladimir Putin's speeches are actually very restrained.

During the Obama administration, conservatives in the U.S. State Department, including Assistant Secretary of State for European Affairs Victoria Nuland and her husband Robert Kagan, founder of the Project for a New American Century, as well as Samantha Power, U.S. Ambassador to the United Nations, and others, have adopted a policy to prod and provoke Putin, and have overtly stated that they want "regime change" in Russia. Predictably, Russia is renewing its nuclear weapons in response, and so is China. Yes, the United States always sets the trend. Donald Trump, perhaps for nefarious reasons, has seemed more inclined to court Putin, which, in a small silver lining for his election as president, may actually defuse the situation in Ukraine and elsewhere.

But we also face proliferation of nuclear weapons in other countries, which could destabilize the balance of terror between Russia and the United States. India and Pakistan each have over a hundred nuclear weapons, because they were sold nuclear power plants which provided them with plutonium fuel that they turned into weapons. India's reactors were constructed with the help of Canada, the United Kingdom, the United States, and Russia, while Pakistan's reactors were sourced with help from Canada and China. Neither of these countries is a signatory of the Treaty on the Non-Proliferation of Nuclear Weapons (NPT), nor is Israel, which is armed with up to two hundred H-bombs. And North Korea, which signed the NPT but withdrew in 2003, might have one or several bombs capable of blowing up a city or two.

But only Russia and America can destroy evolution, and the creation, which makes them the real terrorists of the world. Why don't the European countries stand up to America? Where is their courage? Do they need the American nuclear umbrella, with its potential to exterminate them all?

The global population doesn't realize just how little time exists for our leaders to make a decision about whether or not to use nuclear weapons even today. Former nuclear launch missile officer Bruce Blair wrote, "Russia has shortened the launch time from what it was during the Cold War. Top military command posts in [the] Moscow area can bypass the entire human chain of command, and directly fire by remote control, rockets in silos and on trucks, as far away as Siberia, in 20 minutes."[3] This creates a psychiatric issue: the real problem—the real pathology—in nuclear war planning is nuclear psychosis. In truth, the world is being run by many people who are either sociopaths—brilliant, charming, erudite, with no moral conscience—or others I would label as schizophrenics who suffer from a split between reality and perception of reality. These men have wired the world up like a ticking time bomb ready to explode at any minute. We are faced, therefore, with a fundamentally medical issue.

Cyberwarfare has made the situation worse. People are hacking into the early warning system in the Pentagon, and also in Russia. There are over one thousand verified attempted hacks into the Pentagon system per day. It's not clear if they are all separate people.

It is within the realm of possibility that sixteen-year-old boys—very smart, minimal frontal lobe development, with little moral awareness—might think it a good thing and a bit of fun to blow up the world. Indeed, in 1974 a sixteen-year-old from Britain hacked into the Pentagon network and into Lockheed Missiles and Space Company, in California.

Apparently an order to launch weapons in U.S. missile silos is the length of a tweet.[4] One hundred and forty characters! Missile crews then in turn transmit a short string of computer signals that immediately ignite the rocket engines of hundreds of land-based missiles. There are 440 land-based missiles in America, each armed with one or two hydrogen bombs, each many times larger than the Hiroshima bomb. It takes one minute to ignite the rocket engines—sixty seconds. As Bruce Blair writes, "I practiced it a hundred times. We were called Minutemen. U.S. submarine crews in Trident submarines, they can fire their missiles within 12 minutes."[5] One minute? Twelve minutes? For humans to destroy evolution?

Close encounters between Russian and Western military aircraft have recently increased because of military turmoil in Ukraine, Crimea, and Syria. NATO fighter planes—NATO is totally controlled and organized by America—are provoking Russia and flying close to Russia's borders. In response, Russian warplanes have stepped up provocative overflights above foreign airspace, and they may be armed with nuclear weapons. Both countries are engaging in so-called "muscular interdiction."[6]

Recently a U.S. spy plane, probing Russian borders, was forced to flee into Swedish airspace to escape harassment by Russian fighters.[7] One mistake such as this could trigger a nuclear war. In order to reassure the United States, NATO allies in Eastern Europe have been flying U.S. strategic bombers to the Ukraine area in provocative formations. Apparently they are not armed with nuclear weapons, but there is absolutely no way of knowing whether the bombs on board are nuclear, conventional, or a mix of both. Russia has therefore countered with threats involving its own strategic bombers along U.S. coastal waters.[8] And Putin is said to have put his nuclear weapons on a high state of alert. It is likely that America has done likewise, and China is talking about it too.[9]

America has also been deploying Aegis destroyer ships, which carry antiballistic missiles to the Black Sea, apparently to reassure allies like Romania. These ships also carry dozens of cruise missiles, with conventional warheads, allowing them to reach Moscow; however, the Russians cannot be certain that they do not carry nuclear weapons. America has been ringing Russia, and China, with antimissile bases.[10]

Early-warning teams in the United States receive sensor data at least once a day that require them to urgently assess whether a nuclear attack is under way or whether the alarm is false. Once or twice a week, they need to take a second close look, and occasionally, the attack looks real enough to bring them to the brink of launching. The early-warning team on duty is supposed to take only three minutes, from the arrival of the sensor data, to make a preliminary assessment and to notify top military and civilian leaders if a nuclear attack is occurring. The situation is extremely delicate. The president then has three minutes to make the decision to press the button. National Security Advisor Zbigniew Brzezinski was seconds away from awakening President Jimmy Carter in the middle of the night to inform him the Soviets had launched an all-out nuclear attack . . . and at the last minute discovered it was a false alarm.[11]

As Russian and U.S. relations have now deteriorated to a Cold War level, the risk of a mistaken launch may be even higher than it was during the Cold War. The Russian satellite early-warning system in space, which would notify them of a nuclear attack, has deteriorated, so the Russians have only two to four minutes' lead time with their remaining functional over-the-horizon radar system to know if America has launched a nuclear attack. Putin is rightly very worried, and America is provoking Putin. We physicians know that it is medically contraindicated to threaten a paranoid patient, because he or she may react in a dangerous fashion. Well, it's hard to know, but in Putin's position I would be a touch paranoid, wouldn't you? Once the weapons are launched in America, they take thirty minutes to go from launch to land. The Russians would pick up the attack at the last minute and launch their weapons. "Winning a nuclear war," according to Pentagon documents, means "killing" the other side's weapons. Billions of people dying is called "collateral damage."[12] America's official nuclear policy is to fight and "win" a nuclear war, a policy recently ratified by Obama.

How does one win a nuclear war? First, you "decapitate" Moscow. You send a submarine-launched missile—flight time of eleven minutes—to "take out Moscow" and kill Putin, so Putin can't press the button. Then you launch two hydrogen bombs to land on each Russian missile silo to "kill" the missiles. The Pentagon has then "won" the nuclear war. But because the Russians don't want to "lose the war" and lose their missiles either, they've excavated a big cave in the Ural Mountains that contains a single rocket, and if they think that decapitation is imminent, the rocket is launched and, by computer control, it sends launch signals to all the Russian missiles. That rocket is called the Dead Hand.

In 2015, ninety-two American missile officers, aged between twenty-two and twenty-seven years old and who are programmed like Pavlovian dogs to initiate nuclear war, were suspended because they had been either cheating, taking drugs, or sleeping in the missile silos. Tasked with guarding 150 nuclear missiles at F.E. Warren Air Force Base in Wyoming, fourteen airmen are presently under investigation for allegedly using cocaine. In the same year, three launch officers, known as missileers, pled guilty to using Ecstasy after an investigation into illegal drug possession uncovered roughly one hundred officers involved in a cheating scandal.[13]

In 2013 Vice Admiral Timothy Giardina, the head of the U.S. Strategic Command, was sacked for illegal gambling, and Major General Michael Carey, in charge of the 450 intercontinental ballistic missile silos, was sacked because he went to Moscow, got drunk, insisted that he sing in Russian night clubs, and cavorted with inappropriate women. Clearly we are in the hands of fallible men—fallible human beings armed with missiles and hydrogen bombs that can destroy life on the planet.

There are two officers in each missile silo, each armed with a pistol to shoot the other if he shows signs of deviant behavior. They operate with floppy disks and often their telephones don't work. How are we still here? And no one seems to give a damn. Fidel Castro was obsessed with the distinct possibility of nuclear war in the last years of his life. But none of the 2016 presidential candidates in America discussed this issue. German chancellor Angela Merkel isn't talking about it, and she's the most responsible leader in Europe. Nobody is discussing it, except Putin, who I believe is maintaining a degree of sanity under severe provocation.

This book is designed to provide a realistic assessment of the nuclear threat facing us in the early decades of the twenty-first century. The book is divided into sections on Nuclear Weaponry, Nuclear Politics, and Nuclear Remedies. The first section begins with Seth Baum's relative risk assessment, comparing the two great existential threats facing civilization today: global warming and nuclear weapons. Hans Kristensen provides an overview of the state of the nuclear arsenal in the first decades of the twenty-first century, including the disbursement of nuclear weapons across the nine countries known to have them. Alan Robock describes the way even "limited" nuclear war would create a degree of sunlight-absorbing smoke that would have catastrophic climatic effects around the world. Bruce Gagnon looks at the incredible amount of overkill in the world's nuclear arsenal, which, despite arms-reduction treaties, still exists and poses significant threats, and Bob Alvarez focuses on the manufacture and disposal of plutonium, an issue at the heart of nuclear negotiations, given its role in producing nuclear power as well as weaponry. Max Tegmark explicates the new and frightening implications of weapons systems controlled by artificial intelligence. Hugh Guster-son offers an anthropological look at the changing culture inside nuclear weapons laboratories, where many younger scientists have never experienced a nuclear test explosion except in the comfort of a simulation lab. And finally, Steven Starr, Lynn Eden, and Theodore A. Postol make the threat real by showing us in detail the shocking effects of an imagined future nuclear explosion in Manhattan.

The section on Twenty-First-Century Nuclear Politics starts with Noam Chomsky's look at nuclear brinksmanship beginning in the post–World War II era, through the Cold War, and up to the present. Michael Klare writes of planetary flash points where nuclear war could start. Bill Hartung shines a light on the role of weapons manufacturers and their lobbyists in determining U.S. foreign policy. Richard Broinowski surveys the five "hotspots" around the world where standoffs and proxy wars have the potential to turn nuclear. Julian Borger weighs in on U.S. foreign policy under a Trump administration, and the nuclear dangers posed. Robert Parry provides a deep dive specifically into the United States' deteriorating relationship with Russia, particularly in light of Russia's newly refurbished arsenal. We conclude with Ulrich Kühn's forward-looking assessment of Germany's flirtation with nuclear weapons in reaction to the ascendency of Donald Trump in the United States.

The book ends on what I hope is a constructive note, holding up some of the promising forms of resistance, protest, and remedies to our current nuclear madness early in the twenty-first century. Ray Acheson offers a summary of the progress made at the landmark Vienna Conference at the end of 2014 that effectively shifted the disarmament frame to focus on the humanitarian impact of nuclear weapons. Tim Wright describes the new movement to ban nuclear weapons completely, modeled on the chemical weapons ban. In "Don't Bank on the Bomb," Susi Snyder makes the case for divest-ment from companies, banks, and funds that immorally support or invest in nuclear weapons. David Krieger and Holly Barker both describe the efforts of Marshall Islanders—using their dreadful plight as nuclear victims of U.S. weapons testing—to wage a legal battle against the weapons policies of nuclear-armed countries. And finally, Kennette Benedict succinctly argues for a major revision of the "command and control" aspects of the American Constitution that concentrate the ability to wage nuclear war in the hands of one individual—namely, Donald Trump.

It is my hope that, taken together, these pieces will inspire people to lead an antinuclear revolution, through demonstrations and by educating and threatening their elected representatives that if they do not represent the future survival of their constituents, they will not be reelected. A secondary goal is to pressure the media to report the truth about the nuclear peril to the planet. All this will involve leaving our comfortable chairs and computers, working out brilliant strategies with fellow human beings, and devoting every fiber of our bodies and souls to preserving the wondrous process of evolution and possibly the only life in the universe. This is the ultimate parenting issue: Why make sure our children clean their teeth, get immunized, and acquire a good education if they have no future? Why are we making and selling weapons to exterminate people while up to one billion children are dying of starvation and the effects of polluted water around the globe? Let us stand tall in our human dignity, empathy, and intelligence.

SLEEPWALKING TO ARMAGEDDON

PART ONE

TWENTY-FIRST-CENTURY
NUCLEAR WEAPONRY

1

Assessing Global Catastrophic Risk

Seth D. Baum

Imagine living here on Earth five billion years from now—toward the end of when it is physically possible to live on Earth. The sun gradually gets warmer and, over billions of years, eventually it becomes too hot for life as we know it to survive here on Earth. But five billion years from now, humans might exist not only on Earth; we might have spread across the stars, forming an immense galactic civilization that dwarfs anything we could have on Earth.

What besides the sun could jeopardize the future of the human race? Because humans are currently confined to Earth, major global catastrophes are events so severe that they could make the difference for that entire great, beautiful future of the species. A global catastrophe could ruin it all, depriving countless members of countless future generations the chance ever to live. So, will we succeed at avoiding catastrophe, so that this great, beautiful future can occur? Or will we fail, ruining it all?

When we talk about the catastrophic risk of nuclear war, the biggest thing that could be at stake is no less than the entire fate of human civilization.

We know that a single nuclear weapon can cause an enormous explosion. And we know that the explosion can cause great damage and kill many people. But a single nuclear explosion does not make for a major global catastrophe. It would kill many people, but it would leave the rest of human civilization intact.

In fact, the biggest risk from nuclear weapons is not the initial explosion itself, but the smoke from the firestorm, which would rise high up into the atmosphere and spread out all around the world. This smoke would block incoming sunlight, cooling the surface of the planet and reducing precipitation. The resulting extreme environmental conditions would make it very difficult for plants to grow, including those we grow for our food.

Studies have shown that in a nuclear war scenario with a hundred nuclear weapons, extreme environmental conditions could cause a famine in which two billion people are at risk of starvation. If two billion people die, this would obviously be an enormous catastrophe. But on its own, two billion people dying does not make for a major, permanent global catastrophe. After all, if two billion people die, there are still five billion people alive and able to carry humanity into the future. Needless to say, this doesn't mean that we shouldn't care about two billion people dying. Of course we should care. But, from the perspective of the entire fate of human civilization, two billion deaths might not matter all that much.

So what would matter? Would nuclear war cause the permanent collapse of global human civilization? Throughout human civilization, a number of great civilizations have collapsed, some never to return. And some of these collapses were caused in part by environmental problems. However, none of these civilizations come anywhere close to the scale and sophistication of the modern global civilization we live in today. So it is very difficult to say whether a nuclear war would cause the collapse of global human civilization.

One thing we can say is that the larger the nuclear war, the more likely a permanent collapse. If zero nuclear weapons are used and there is no nuclear war, there is no chance of permanent catastrophe. If all sixteen thousand nuclear weapons that exist in the world today are used, the probability of permanent catastrophe is high. Exactly how high is uncertain, but high enough for us to worry about. On the other hand, we can imagine a nuclear war that entailed, say, thirty or forty nuclear weapons. If they're dropped on major cities, major nodes in the global economy, there would be large global economic and political consequences, but the environmental risks would probably be small. Indeed, at a threshold of about fifty nuclear weapons, the probability of permanent catastrophe from the environmental consequences is insignificantly low, so low that at that point we have more important things to worry about, including all the other catastrophic risks. There is still the chance of permanent catastrophe from the loss of major cities causing global economic failure. In this case, the threshold might be lower than fifty nuclear weapons, but it is still somewhere above zero.

Even if human civilization can survive into the distant future with thirty or fifty nuclear weapons, there are still plenty of good reasons to aim for a world with zero nuclear weapons. But the important thing is not the difference between zero and fifty nuclear weapons, but the difference between either of those and the sixteen thousand weapons in the world today. It is imperative both that these weapons not be used, and that their number be reduced down to a safe level, because these weapons pose a catastrophic risk to the species.

In addition to assessing the impacts of nuclear war entailing different numbers of weapons, a complete treatment of risk also needs to look at the probability of nuclear war occurring. If the probability is zero, then there will be no nuclear war, and we don't have to worry about the consequences. And indeed, there are some people who would say that the probability basically is zero. After all, there have never been any nuclear wars before.

Well, that isn't quite true. There has been a nuclear war; World War II was a nuclear war. But it is true that there has never been a large nuclear war involving fifty or sixteen thousand nuclear weapons. However, the fact that no large nuclear war has ever happened before doesn't mean that the probability one will happen in the future is zero.

This is the same mistake that people in Britain made several centuries ago about black swans. They believed that black swans were impossible. They had never seen black swans before. To them, all swans were white. But there are black swans. They live in Australia. It is a mistake to believe something is impossible just because you've never seen it before.

There is an additional reason this kind of thinking is a mistake with respect to nuclear war—researchers call it the observation selection effect. We are selected to observe only those events that do not kill us. If a large enough nuclear war could kill us all, then we can observe it only in the brief moment when we are dying. The fact that you're alive today reading this book requires that no such large nuclear war has ever occurred before. So it is that much more of a mistake to say that the probability is zero just because we've never seen it happen before.

So, what can we say?

One thing we can do is look at the history we have observed and learn what we can from that. For example, the Cuban Missile Crisis is perhaps the closest the world has ever come to nuclear war. Martin Hellman of Stanford University modeled the series of steps through which crises like the Cuban Missile Crisis could end in nuclear war. First is the relative calm before the crisis. Second is the initiating event, which in Cuba was the United States' discovery of Soviet nuclear weapons there. Third is the crisis itself. Fourth is the launch of a nuclear weapon. Finally, fifth is the escalation to full-scale nuclear war. The first three steps all occurred in the Cuban Missile Crisis. The fourth and fifth steps have not previously occurred but would need to occur for the crisis to end in nuclear war.

For each of the steps in the model, Hellman estimated the probability of its going on to the next step. For the first two probabilities, he used numbers based on observations from history. For the second two probabilities, he used a range of numbers. The steps have never happened before, so the probability of getting there is uncertain. Multiplying these numbers out gives a range of probabilities corresponding to about one of these nuclear wars occurring every two hundred years to one per five thousand years.

Once per two hundred or five thousand years might seem like a low-probability rare event. And it's true: this type of nuclear war is unlikely to happen this year, or next year, or the year after that. But the longer we wait, the further into the future we go, the more likely it is for one of these nuclear wars to occur. And it is highly improbable—basically impossible—that with weapon supplies remaining at their current levels, humanity could make it for billions of years into the distant future without one of these nuclear wars occurring. And this analysis is just for an intentional nuclear war.

Another type of nuclear war is called inadvertent nuclear war. Inadvertent nuclear war occurs when one side misinterprets a false alarm as a real nuclear attack and launches nuclear weapons in what it believes is a counterattack but which is in fact the first strike. Inadvertent nuclear war is important because it means we could end up in nuclear war even if deterrence works perfectly.

What is deterrence? Deterrence is threatening someone else with some sort of harm in order to convince them to not do something. In nuclear deterrence, both sides threaten each other with nuclear retaliation. Since neither side wants to be hit with that retaliation, neither side launches their nuclear weapons. It's a way of avoiding nuclear war. And deterrence works. However, it does not work perfectly. This is shown by a number of historical cases, including the Cuban Missile Crisis.

Even if deterrence did work perfectly, we could still end up in an inadvertent nuclear war. In the inadvertent nuclear war scenario, the other side actually was deterred. They had not launched nuclear weapons. But the one side thought they were under attack anyway, and we end up in nuclear war.

Over the years, there have been a number of close calls of inadvertent nuclear war. These are false alarms that were believed to be real nuclear attacks. Here are five of them:

- November 1979: The United States' North American Aerospace Defense Command (NORAD) training tapes appear to show a real Soviet strike.
- June 1980: U.S. Strategic Air Command has a faulty computer chip showing Soviet missile launches.
- September 1983: Sunlight reflects off clouds toward a Soviet monitoring satellite, triggering an alarm. Soviet Air Defense Forces officer Stanislav Petrov refuses to treat the alarm as real.
- November 1983: NATO begins a large military exercise in Western Europe. Some of the Soviet leadership believe the exercise is cover for a real attack, and in response the Soviets put their nuclear forces on alert.
- January 1995: Russia detects a joint USA-Norway scientific rocket launch off Norway's coast, believing it to be a nuclear missile.

Fortunately, in each of these cases, no nuclear weapons were used. However, in the future, we might not be so fortunate.

My colleagues and I have studied the probability of inadvertent nuclear war between the United States and Russia using what's called a fault tree model. A fault tree branches out into different scenarios, each of which could be at fault for causing inadvertent nuclear war.

The leaves at the ends of the branches are two types of false alarms and two conditions in which the alarms can occur. One type of alarm is the "usual" alarm, which are the sorts of false alarms that have happened before, as discussed earlier. The other type is a nuclear terrorist attack misinterpreted as an attack by another country. The two conditions are crisis conditions between the two countries and conditions of relative calm. As you might imagine, countries are a lot more likely to believe they are actually under attack if they are in a crisis.

We modeled the series of steps going from the alarm, through the chain of command, to the ultimate decision to launch nuclear weapons in response. The chain of command goes from the military staff who monitor for false alarms, to their superiors, all the way up to the president, who makes the launch decision. For each step, we considered a range of probabilities for the alarm being passed to the next step. We also used a range for the probability of crisis between the countries. We used ranges because the exact numbers are uncertain.

Multiplying these out gives a range of results for the probability of United States–Russia inadvertent nuclear war. We looked at two cases: if the war can happen at any time or if it can happen only during a crisis. We get wide ranges for each: once per fourteen years to once per five thousand years if it can happen at any time, and once per twenty years or once per hundred thousand years if it can happen only during a crisis. The ranges are so wide because it is such an uncertain risk.

Despite the uncertainty, the numbers clearly show that this is a worrisome risk. The average probabilities are fifty and one hundred years. Even with the low probabilities, once per five thousand and hundred thousand years, a catastrophe is likely to occur not too far into the distant future.

One thing we can see in the inadvertent nuclear war numbers is that the probability of inadvertent nuclear war is lower if it can happen only during crisis. This shows that we can reduce the risk by avoiding crisis. That means resolving the current conflict in Ukraine, which has increased tensions between the United States and Russia. It means making sure tensions over Taiwan never escalate between the United States and China. And so on for other issues between other nuclear-armed countries.

Indeed, a core reason it's important to analyze risks in so much detail is because at every step along the way we learn of opportunities to reduce the risks, and we get some understanding for how effective they would be.

So how do we get to the great, beautiful future that human civilization can enjoy without destroying it all with a major global catastrophe? The answer is by understanding the risks and seizing the opportunities we have to reduce them. For the sake of the entire future of human civilization, we should make these activities a top priority.

2

Modernization of Nuclear Weaponry

Hans Kristensen

The good news is that enormous progress has been made since the Cold War in terms of reducing the overall arsenals. Those people who lived and worked during that period will remember that literally the entire world lived thirty minutes from annihilation every single day—it was frontline news, in your face all the time, and not just hypothetical. Nuclear weapons were literally rubbing up against each other—ships and aircraft were loaded with them. Tactical nuclear weapons were on frigates and destroyers sailing all around the world. Those weapons were built to fight other frigates and destroyers and were deployed everywhere. The United States used to have nuclear artillery that could shoot a few tens of kilometers out to destroy some tank columns—battlefield weapons.

Since then we've had an enormous reduction in the number of nuclear weapons, down to approximately 9,400 nuclear weapons in the global military stockpiles—which excludes the thousands more retired, but still intact, warheads awaiting dismantlement. The total inventory has come down, and U.S. and Russian weapons deployed on strategic delivery systems like missiles and long-range bombers—ready to be launched on very short notice—have come down significantly too compared to the 1980s.

But we are still far from moving out of the Cold War mind-set in terms of the arsenals. Even if you believe that nuclear weapons play an important role in national security, the arsenals that exist today

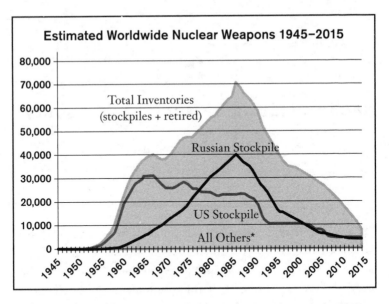

Figure 2.1. More than 125,000 nuclear warheads have been produced since 1945. Nuclear stockpiles peaked in 1986 with 70,300 warheads. Russia and the United States possess 94 percent of the global inventory of nuclear weapons.

*Includes Britain, China, France, India, Israel, North Korea, and Pakistan.

are vastly in excess of what might be considered necessary. There are also large inventories of weapons that have been retired but are still intact. They're working on dismantling those weapons every year, but the military says some portion of them are still necessary.

What's really striking is how disproportionately greater the number of nuclear weapons the United States and Russia feel they need for their security is compared to those of any other country in the world. There are no other countries in the world that say they need more than a couple of hundred nuclear weapons for their security. But the United States and Russia still have enormous arsenals. As a result, they have a special responsibility to reduce those forces to lower levels.

And while we've come down significantly compared to during the Cold War, in the last decade or so the pace of reductions has slowed down. What we see now is the nuclear-weapon states gearing up for the long haul, figuring out what they need to sustain themselves indefinitely as big nuclear powers. So the trend is more a leveling off of the force level, rather than a continuation of the reductions toward zero.

In the United States, the debate has shifted from efforts to reduce the nuclear arsenals to efforts to modernize what's left. During the Obama administration, arms *control* was almost entirely replaced by nuclear arms modernization. Over the next decade, the United States alone plans to spend something on the order of $350 billion on maintaining and modernizing its nuclear forces.[1] Russia and all the other nuclear-weapon states are also modernizing instead of further reducing stockpiles.

Nuclear weapons are typically classified as strategic and nonstrategic (or "tactical"). Strategic weapons are typically larger and deployed from farther away, targeting sites in the interior of an enemy nation. Nonstrategic shorter-range nuclear weapons can be deployed alongside conventional weapons in a battlefield setting. In Europe, where Russia and NATO are in a dispute over Ukraine, this category of weapon is being drawn into the conflict, even if in an unintended way. Because nonstrategic nuclear weapons are typically mounted on so-called dual-capable forces—aircraft or ground launch missiles that can launch conventional weapons as well—it can be difficult to discern whether a weapon on a dual-capable launcher is nuclear or not. In a crisis like the one triggered by the Russian invasion of Ukraine, where Russia is deploying forces to Crimea as well as aircraft into the Baltic Sea, the Norwegian Sea, the North Sea, and the Black Sea, NATO is responding by sending aircraft on a rotational basis into Poland and Romania. Some of those aircraft are dual-capable forces.

Even if NATO doesn't intend to signal that it's deploying tactical nuclear weapons, Russia sees forces that *can* carry nuclear weapons and responds in kind. This has the effect of unintentionally escalating the crisis. We see in the news all the time these days stories

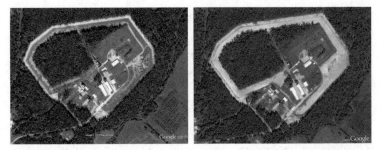

Figure 2.2. Satellite view of the Russian nuclear storage facility at Kaliningrad in May 2007. **Figure 2.3.** The same Russian nuclear facility at Kaliningrad in July 2007. The perimeter around a former nuclear storage site has been updated and cleaned up. Source: Digital Globe via Google Earth.

about Russia deploying nuclear weapons to Crimea. There have been nuclear-capable forces in Crimea for decades. But the framing of their presence is changing, and the new context is feeding into the fear and the perception of how serious the crisis is.

Many of the Russian military forces are dual-capable, serving nonnuclear missions as well. But satellite photos taken over a period of two years reveal updates to the western air bases where they store or operate these weapons, including a medium-range bomber called the Backfire. What the satellite photos reveal is a nuclear weapon storage site, where the perimeter has been modernized and cleaned out, with new fences put in, and the facilities themselves inside being upgraded. It's an active site. Nuclear-weapon states look at each other via these satellite photos.

In Kaliningrad, a similar thing has happened. The perimeter around a former nuclear storage site has been updated and cleaned up—a signal not necessarily that there are nuclear weapons at that storage site, but that they have the capacity to bring them in, if necessary. These actions are used to signal back and forth all the time.

The United States stores about 180 nuclear bombs in Europe: tactical gravity bombs. They are located at six bases in five countries: Belgium, Germany, Italy, the Netherlands, and Turkey.

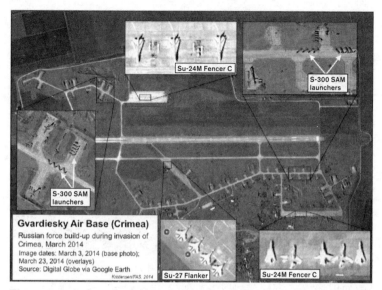

Figure 2.4. A photo from 2014, shortly after the Russians invaded Ukraine and took Crimea, shows Russian deployment of S-300 surface-to-air missile systems and Su-24 bombers in Crimea. Because they are dual capable, nonstrategic nuclear forces such as these are quickly drawn into conflicts. Source: Digital Globe via Google Earth.

France also has air-launched cruise missiles, which they call strategic but which share the same characteristics as Russian weapon types described as tactical. There are plenty of these forces in both Western and Eastern Europe. This is how countries "signal" with tactical nuclear weapons. A photo from 2014, shortly after the Russians invaded Ukraine and took Crimea, shows an air base where a nuclear-capable air defense system moved in literally a couple of days after the invasion. There are nuclear-capable bombers on that base as well.

Another photo shows German air force personnel loading an American B61 nuclear weapon onto a German aircraft. Germany has signed the nonproliferation treaty and has pledged not to receive nuclear weapons, directly or indirectly. Yet, here is a member of the German air force loading an American nuclear bomb

Figure 2.5. German personnel loading a U.S. B61 onto a German Tornado. Germany has signed the nonproliferation treaty and has pledged not to receive nuclear weapons, directly or indirectly.

onto a German plane. This is part of the nuclear sharing arrangement we still have in NATO, where allied countries are given missions to deliver American nuclear weapons in times of war.

Another satellite photo, not shown here, shows the 510th Fighter Squadron from Aviano airbase in Italy, forward deployed to Lask Air Base in Poland. This is a nuclear-capable fighter squadron moving into Poland. The Russians see this and it goes to their perception of what NATO is doing. At the same time NATO is saying this is not about nuclear weapons, it's being viewed by the Russians as a nuclear threat. Another photo shows a French Mirage aircraft intercepting a Russian Backfire bomber over the Baltic Sea. These things happen every day, all the time. And they are happening more because of the crisis in Ukraine and the responses to it.

In a snapshot of the world's forces, where are countries that have nuclear weapons today putting their emphasis? It is not on the elimination of nuclear weapons. It is not on implementing Article

Nuclear Modernization: Russia

ICBM
- SS-27 Mod 2 (mobile): replacing SS-25s at Novosibirsk, Tagil, Yoshkar-Ola
- SS-27 Mod 2 (silo): replacing SS-19s at Kozelsk
- SS-27 Mod 2 (rail): planned
- RS-26 (compact SS-27): to replace SS-25s at Irkutsk and Vypolzovo
- Sarmat "heavy ICBM": to replace SS-28s at Dombarovsky and Uzhur

SSBN / SLBM
- SS-N-23 SLBM life-extension (Sineva/Layner) in Delta IV SSBN
- Borey SSBN: 8 planned (possibly 10-12)
- SS-N-32 (Bulava): fielding

Bombers
- Upgrades of some Tu-160 (Blackjack) and Tu-95 (Bear)
- New bomber (PAK PA) in development
- ALCM (Kh-102) in development

Tactical
- Tu-22M (Backfire) upgrade under way
- Su-34 (Fullback) fielding*
- Yasen (Sverodvinsk) SSGN in development
- SLCM (SS-N-30, Kaliber) in development
- GLCM test-launched; in production?**
- SSM (SS-26, Iskander) deploying
- SAM (S-400/SA-21) deploying (nuclear?)
- ABM (A-135) upgrade planned

*"Fielding" means the weapons are being introduced into the military forces.

**A question mark on these tables indicates that this is rumored but unverified.

Source: Hans Kristensen, Federation of American Scientists, 2015.

Nuclear Modernization: United States

ICBM
- Minuteman III life-extension completing
- Warhead fuzes/interoperable warhead planned
- GBSD (ICBM replacement) in development

SSBN / SLBM
- Trident II D5 SLBM life-extension in development
- SSBN replacement in development (12 planned)
- W76-1 warhead life-extension deploying
- W88-1 warhead life-extension development

Bombers
- Upgrade of B-2 and B-52 under way
- LRS-B next-generation bomber in development
- B61-12 guided standoff bomb in development
- LRSO (ALCM) replacement in development

Tactical
- F-35A nuclear capability in development
- B61-12 guided standoff in development

Infrastructure
- Uranium Processing Facility (secondaries) in construction
- Plutonium production facilities (primaries) in construction
- Warhead surveillance/simulation facilities upgrade

Source: Hans Kristensen, Federation of American Scientists, 2015.

Six under the Non-Proliferation Treaty, which commits the nuclear armed states to end the nuclear arms race and negotiate to reduce and eventually eliminate nuclear weapons. Instead, the emphasis is on modernizing and extending their nuclear arsenals. In Russia, upgrades and modernization of the country's nuclear forces is happening across the board. ICBMs, sea-launched ballistic missiles, bombers, and tactical nuclear weapons systems are all being modernized. In the United States, ICBMs, submarines, ballistic mis-

Nuclear Modernization: France

SSBN / SLBM
- TNO warhead on M51.2 SLBM
- M51.3 SLBM development

Bombers
- Rafale K3 planned at Istres Air Base
- Next-generation ALCM in development

Infrastucture
- Megajoule at CESTA in development
- Airix/Epure hydrodynamic test center at Valduc in development (partly Joint French-UK warhead surveillance testing center)

Source: Hans Kristensen, Federation of American Scientists, 2015.

siles, bombers, tactical nuclear weapons, infrastructure, nuclear weapons production facilities across the board are being upgraded.

In a few years we will see the introduction of America's first nuclear "guided" bomb. We don't have a guided nuclear bomb in the arsenal today, but the B61 is being upgraded with a guided tail kit so that it can hit its target more accurately. In the early 2020s those weapons will be deployed to Europe.

In France, the same thing is happening: France is modernizing. This year it's putting a new warhead on its sea-launched ballistic missiles at sea. It has a bomber fleet of Mirage and Dassault Rafale fighters that have nuclear cruise missiles that have been upgraded. France has also been upgrading its warhead maintenance infrastructure.

In Britain, there is also modernization, although at a lower level; they have fewer forces left. But Britain is about to build a new class of ballistic missile submarines, four of them. The United States is building the missile launch component for them, and is supplying the missiles as well as the reentry vehicle containing the nuclear warhead.

Nuclear Modernization: Britain

SSBN / SLBM
- SSBN (Vanguard replacement) in development (3-4 planned)
- SLBM (Trident II D5LE) in development (USA)
- Mk4A/W76-1 type warhead fielding

Infrastructure
- Joint UK-French warhead surveillance testing technology center in development

Source: Hans Kristensen, Federation of American Scientists, 2015.

Nuclear Modernization: China

ICBM / MRBM
- DF-31A (CSS-10 Mod 2) deploying
- New mobile ICBM test-launching
- New mobile ICBM capable of delivering MIRV in development

SSBN / SLBM
- Jin (Type-094) SSBN fielding (4-5 expected)
- JL-2 (CSS-N-14) SLBM in development
- Type-096 SSBN possibly in development

Cruise Missiles
- ALCM (CJ-20 on H-6 bomber) in development*
- GLCM (DH-10/CJ-10) fielding**

Note: China is the only one of the P-5 (NPT declared) nuclear armed states that is increasing its nuclear arsenal.
* Listed in 2013 AFGSC briefing
** Listed by NASIC as "conventional or nuclear," the same designation as the Russian nuclear-capable AS-4 Kitchen ALCM

Source: Hans Kristensen, Federation of American Scientists, 2015.

Nuclear Modernization: Pakistan

MRBM / SRBM
- Shaheen II MRBM (Haz-6) fielding
- NASR SRBM (Haz-9) in development
- Abdali SRBM (Haz-2) in development*

Cruise Missiles
- GLCM (Babur/Haz-7) in development
- ALCM (Ra'ad/Haz-8 on Mirage) in development
- SLCM (naval version of Babur) in development?

Infrastructure
- Khushab-IV reactor #4 in construction
- Uranium enrichment facility upgrade

* Listed by Pakistani ISPR but not by 2013 NASIC report

Source: Hans Kristensen, Federation of American Scientists, 2015.

China—a country with a minimum deterrence strategy—is implementing a broad modernization as well. They're introducing new ICBMs. They have two new systems that are apparently being developed, one of them possibly with multiple warheads. The Chinese also have a new class of sea-launched ballistic missile submarines that are coming in with a new missile, and cruise missiles that are rumored to have nuclear capability. These missiles are going on the bombers and on ground-launch systems.

The United States, Russia, and France are reducing their arsenals but also modernizing them. China, Pakistan, and India are *increasing* their arsenals. Pakistan probably has the fastest-growing nuclear arsenal in the world, and now short- and medium-range ballistic missiles are being added. Pakistan has a very short-range rocket or ballistic missile, with a range of only sixty kilometers. This is a system that Pakistan is specifically talking about using in a tactical nuclear weapons fashion, that the military is *actually considering*

Nuclear Modernization: India

ICBM / IRBM / MRBM
- Agni VI ICBM in development (MIRV?)
- Agni V ICBM in development
- Agni IV IRBM in development
- Agni III IRBM fielding

SSBN / SLBM
- Arihant SSBN in development (3+ expected)
- K-15/K-4 SLBM in development
- Dhanush SLBM in development

Cruise Missiles
- GLCM (Nirbhay) in development*

Infrastructure
- Two plutonium production reactors in development

* Reported by news media but not listed in 2013 NASIC report

Source: Hans Kristensen, Federation of American Scientists, 2015.

using in scenarios below the "big scenario," most likely in response to a conventional attack from India. These are two countries that have been at war many times over the last fifty years, which raises serious questions about the potential use of nuclear weapons in that region. Pakistan is also building plutonium production facilities and air- and ground-launch cruise missiles. It has a very broad nuclear program.

In India, we see the same thing, although India is now shifting attention more from Pakistan toward China. So we are beginning to see India build more longer-range ballistic missiles that can reach and cover all of China. In early 2015 we saw an Agni 5 Intermediate Range Ballistic Missile launched from a new kind of launcher, which is a canister. Previously the Indians have transported their missiles on these open launchers. Now they're going

Nuclear Modernization: Israel

IRBM
- Jericho III IRBM in development?

SSG / SLBM
- Dolphin SSG fielding
- SLCM (Popeye Turbo/Harpoon) rumored*

Bomber
- F-35A acquisition

* Reported by news media but denied by officials. US public intelligence reports omit references to Israeli nuclear forces

Source: Hans Kristensen, Federation of American Scientists, 2015.

to incorporate them into these canisters, which will enable them to become more mobile and flexible, and also to launch faster. They're building a ballistic missile submarine, as well as equipping it with ballistic missiles, and there are rumors that they're working on a cruise missile. Plutonium production reactors are also in design and construction.

Israel has a very opaque nuclear arsenal. It doesn't confirm its existence. But it's known that they have nuclear weapons, and that they've had them since the 1970s. They have at least two types of nuclear launchers. The first is a longer-range version of the ballistic missile. They might have equipped their submarines with nuclear capabilities; we're not quite sure but there are certainly rumors. The Israelis also have bombers, and they are acquiring the F-35A joint-strike fighter from the United States. In other countries this aircraft is equipped with nuclear capability when it's deployed. We don't know what its status is going to be in the Israeli air force, but it could be used in a nuclear role.

As of May 2017, North Korea has conducted five nuclear tests and

---

Nuclear Modernization: North Korea*

CBM / IRBM / MRBM
- No Dong MRBM fielding
- Musudan IRBM in development
- Hwasong-13 (KN-08) ICBM in development (fielding?)
- Taepo Dong 2 SLV/ICBM in development

Cruise Missiles
- KN-09 coastal defense cruise missile in development ?**

Infrastructure
- Yongbyon plutonium production reactor re-start
- Uranium enrichment production construction

* Despite three underground nuclear tests in 2013, there is no known public evidence that North Korea has miniaturized its test devices sufficiently for delivery by ballistic missiles
** Listed by 2013 AFGSC briefing but not in 2013 NASIC report. 2014 update of AFGSC does not list KN-09.

Source: Hans Kristensen, Federation of American Scientists, 2015.

is trying to build operational nuclear weapons. We see medium-range missiles, intermediate-range missiles, ICBMs, and all sorts of other things being described by the intelligence community. The big unknown is whether North Korea has a nuclear warhead that it can deliver with a missile. The Korean government acts as if it does, and talks as if it does, but there is no public evidence that North Korea has improved its nuclear test devices sufficiently to deliver them with a ballistic missile. We just don't know; they're certainly trying.

Then there is NATO, not a nuclear-weapon state, but an alliance that relies heavily on nuclear weapons. Five of the twenty-eight countries in NATO have nuclear strike mission capacity with American nuclear weapons: the Germans, the Dutch, Belgians, Italians, and possibly the Turks.

Nuclear Modernization: NATO

- Modification of B61 bomb from "dumb" bomb to guided, standoff B61-12 with guided tail kit assembly that increases targeting accuracy and effciency
  - Integration on F-15E in 2013-2018
  - Integration on F-16 in 2015-2018
  - Integration on PA-200 in 2015-2017
  - First Production Unit in 2020

- Addition of nuclear-capability to F-35A II Lightning fighter-bomber
  - Integration of B61-12 in 2015-2021
  - Delivery to Italy, the Netherlands, and Turkey (and Israel?)

- B61-12 will also be integrated onto strategic bombers (B-2 and new LRS-B)

- Upgrade of storage sites and handling

- B61-12 cost: more than a decade worth of European Reassurance Initiatives

Source: Hans Kristensen, Federation of American Scientists, 2015.

And now NATO is developing a new weapon: the guided B61 upgrade. It is a new weapon because a guided nuclear bomb does not exist in the United States today. The spin we hear from the U.S. government is: "Oh no, it's not a new weapon. We've just painted the old one. We've just brushed off the dust from wherever, and it's just coming back as a life-extended warhead." But it is a new nuclear weapon because it has added new capabilities. The B61 will go on the stealthy F-35A joint strike fighter starting in the early 2020s in Europe. It will also arm the American strategic bombers in the United States. So you'll have the same bomb deployed on tactical aircraft and strategic aircraft. Flight-testing of this prototype is going on right now. And over the next three years they're going to integrate this weapon on five different aircraft: the F-35, the F-15E, the F-16, the European Tornado, and the B-2 bomber. It will go on the next long-range-strike bomber as well.

There has been a lot of talk about disarmament, a lot of talk about putting an end to Cold War thinking. But this talk does not seem to be reflected in what's happening with nuclear forces worldwide. There's no indication that the role of nuclear weapons has been significantly reduced in recent years. In fact, the role of nuclear weapons today, the core mission, is exactly as it has always been: to hold at risk adversaries' targets, and draw up the plans so that if deterrence fails, the military can destroy those targets.

The idea behind this is that you scare an adversary into not doing the bad things they plan to do. But it becomes a sort of self-fulfilling cycle: you keep having to make forces credible. You keep having to modernize the forces; otherwise the other side will not believe you can do what you say you can. Right now we're seeing the arms control and disarmament side losing to the momentum of nuclear weapons modernization plans. This is not in terms of numbers of weapons—we're not talking about Cold War–style huge arsenal buildups. Instead, we're seeing an endless, indefinite, and sustained nuclear technological competition that is going on as we speak between all the nuclear weapon states.

What we need are new initiatives that break this pattern, that try not only to continue the reductions of nuclear forces, but also to create changes in the way countries that have nuclear weapons envision their potential use. The cycle has to be broken or there's no way out. It's an infinite loop.

3

Nuclear Smoke and the Climatic Effects of Nuclear War

Alan Robock

Although the Cold War and its associated arms race are over, new calculations show that the current world arsenal of about sixteen thousand nuclear weapons (as of August 2014) could still produce a nuclear winter that would last for a decade or more, much longer than was originally thought. Meanwhile, the number of countries with nuclear weapons increased at a rate of about one every five years over the course of the Cold War, with two more added since the breakup of the Soviet Union. We now have nine nuclear nations. If two of the new nuclear nations—say, India and Pakistan—were to engage in a regional nuclear conflict involving a much smaller number of nuclear weapons, the result might not be "winter," with below-freezing temperatures. But recent computer models show that the impact on the planet—not just the nations at war—would still be terribly dire: millions would die from the blast effects, radioactivity, and fires, and there would be severe impacts on global agriculture for more than a decade.

To understand the climatic effects of such a regional war, we did a simulation targeting one hundred Hiroshima-sized weapons (15 kT) on the fifty targets in each of the two countries that would produce the largest amount of smoke if attacked.[1] India would produce 3.5 million tons of smoke and Pakistan, 3 million tons, but to be conservative, we simulated the effects of 5 million tons of smoke. What would be the human toll and what would be the climate

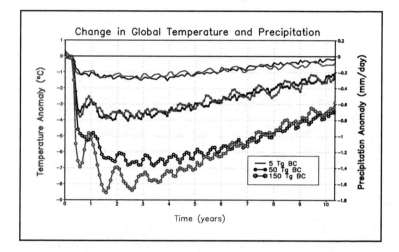

Figure 3.1. The modeled effects on surface weather (SW) of a nuclear explosion of a 5-Tg (Teragram, or a million tons) bomb (top), a 50-Tg bomb (middle), and a 150-Tg bomb (bottom).[2]

response to putting 5 million tons of smoke into the upper atmosphere, accounting for fuel loading, emission factors, and rainout? We used the NASA Goddard Institute for Space Studies climate model to simulate the climate response.

Nuclear war would have two types of targets: air and ground bursts. Both would result in fires and put smoke in the atmosphere. Cities would burn and firestorms would build. Ground bursts also produce dust. In the case of air bursts, sunlight gets absorbed; in ground bursts it gets reflected. But both mean that very little sunlight would reach the ground, and that would cause rapid large drops in surface temperature. This would be devastating to agriculture and natural ecosystems. The smoke in the atmosphere would heat the upper atmosphere, which would then destroy ozone, and that would mean a lot more ultraviolet radiation reaching the ground, which would be devastating for life. These conditions would produce cold, dry, dark conditions at the surface but also more ultraviolet light, killing crops and producing global famine.

We used the same kinds of models we use for weather prediction and climate simulations, but never want to test our theories in the real world. Therefore we also used analogues that inform us about parts of the story. We know it gets cold in the winter when the sun is not as intense. We know it gets colder at night. So we have a feeling for how cold it can get if we turn off the sun. We have examples of cities burning, both in San Francisco after the earthquake, and during World War II from so-called "conventional" bombs. We have examples from volcanic eruptions and Martian dust storms, with dust and smoke being transported around the world and causing cooling. And these phenomena inform our models.

In terms of immediate impact on human life, in the short term, twenty million people would die from direct effects—half the total fatalities from all of World War II. Portions of megacities attacked with nuclear devices or exposed to fallout of long-lived isotopes would likely have to be abandoned indefinitely.

On the climate front, the smoke would take its toll over a period of time. On day one, most of the sooty smoke in the troposphere would be heated and rise up into the stratosphere, where there wouldn't be any rain to wash it out. It would stay there for over a decade, covering the entire world. For the scenario of an India-Pakistan war, there would not be enough smoke to create winter temperatures, but it would make the planet a couple of degrees Celsius colder—colder than the Little Ice Age—which would be climate change unprecedented in recorded human history.

Two other climate models—a Swiss model, and one produced by the National Center for Atmospheric Research (NCAR)—have recently done a similar calculation, finding basically the same result.[3] In the NCAR model, which is much more detailed and also includes the effects of ozone, as with other models, the smoke goes up, gets heated, and goes into the upper stratosphere, where it stays for years.

Our first calculation showed that the global temperature would go down by 1.5 degrees Celsius, about 3 degrees Fahrenheit. The Swiss model showed similar results. The NCAR model, which calculated more detail, showed the smoke lasting longer—for a couple of decades—and a little more cooling. What difference does a couple of degrees make? We looked at places where food is grown and applied the change of temperature, the change of precipitation, and the change of sunlight to calculate the impact on crops and on oceans.

In China—the country that grows the most food—in the first five years following a regional nuclear war between India and Pakistan, rice production would be down by 20 percent and winter wheat production would be down by 40 percent, resulting in the same amount of food that was grown in China when the country had several hundred million fewer people.[4] In the United States, corn production would go down by 20 percent, soybeans by 15 percent, and rice by 25 percent.[5] Imagine people hoarding food, world food trade collapsing. The same would be true for every country in the world—a regional nuclear conflict would have devastating consequences for every person on the planet, not just the countries at war.

Larger weapons would produce even more smoke, with worse climatic consequences. A Trident submarine has 96 nuclear weapons, each 100 or 475 kT—much more powerful than the Hiroshima bomb. Each Trident submarine can produce the equivalent of about a thousand Hiroshimas. The United States has fourteen Trident submarines, and that's only half of our arsenal. The Russians have as many nuclear weapons. We did a simulation of what would happen if the United States and Russia had a nuclear war.[6] A lot more smoke would go up in the atmosphere. It would cause much greater temperature change: 7 to 8 degrees Celsius colder.

(The amount of smoke generated in this model is the same amount we saw when we were studying nuclear winter in the 1980s, with models that used a third of the then-much-larger arsenals. It turns out that, during the Cold War, with only a third of the arsenals, every possible target in Russia and the United States had nine nuclear bombs targeted on it. This represented a huge number of excess weapons. Today, even after the New START agreement, if we put one nuclear weapon on each target, our model still produces the same amount of smoke.)

Thus a nuclear war between *any* nuclear states, using much less than 1 percent of the current nuclear arsenal, could produce climate change unprecedented in recorded human history. Such a "small" nuclear war could reduce food production by 20–40 percent for a decade. And the current Russian and American arsenals can still produce complete nuclear winter, with temperatures below freezing for more than a decade.

In the 1980s, the climate model simulations were done on a Cray-1 computer, which is much less powerful than an iPhone in terms of computing capability and storage. Now we have modern models that can heat the smoke, model the upper atmosphere, and calculate how long the smoke would stay there. What we discovered was not that we were wrong about the dangers, but that we had underestimated them.

In the 1980s, scientists first produced models showing that the effect of nuclear war would be a devastating change in climate, which they termed "nuclear winter." Leaders at the time recognized the threat and took the first steps to mitigate the danger. Mikhail Gorbachev, then head of the Soviet Union, later reflected, "Models made by Russian and American scientists showed that a nuclear war would result in a nuclear winter that would be extremely destructive to all life on Earth; the knowledge of that was a great stimulus to us, to people of honor and morality, to act in that situation."[7]

More recently, President Obama and President Medvedev signed the New START Treaty in 2010. New START pledged that within seven years, each side would bring their nuclear warheads down to 1,550 per side. But in the strange calculations of diplomacy, each nuclear bomber counted as one nuclear weapon because they couldn't tell how many bombs there were inside of them. Both countries would still have about two thousand nuclear weapons each. That's four thousand nuclear warheads altogether, maybe another thousand in the rest of the world. A far better policy would be immediate reductions in the American and Russian arsenals to the size of those of the other nuclear nations, about two hundred each, in order to eliminate the threat of nuclear winter. In that situation, we wouldn't be able to produce enough smoke to actually cause temperatures to go below freezing and sentence the entire world to famine.

But, if we want to prevent the famine that would result from a nuclear war between India and Pakistan, where perhaps a billion people would die because of reduction in the food supply, we would have to get rid of *all* nuclear weapons. Carl Sagan, as far back as the 1980s, said: "For myself, I would far rather have a world in which the climatic catastrophe cannot happen, independent of the vicissitudes of leaders, institutions, and machines. This seems to me to be elementary planetary hygiene. As well as elementary patriotism."[8]

Elementary planetary hygiene demands that we eliminate the nuclear weapons much faster than they're being eliminated now. We've banned biological weapons, chemical weapons, land mines, and cluster munitions. But the worst weapons of mass destruction of all, nuclear weapons, have not been banned. Now the International Campaign Against Nuclear Weapons (ICAN) is working to ban them. You can choose to work with them toward this end because, as Dr. Seuss sagely wrote: "Unless someone like you cares a whole awful lot, nothing's gonna get better, it's not."[9]

4

Addicted to Weapons

Bruce Gagnon

I live in Bath, Maine, where navy destroyers are built. These ships are outfitted with so-called "missile defense" systems that the Pentagon is today using to help encircle Russia and China. Few people in our community, including activists, are interested in where these ships go or what their military mission is. It's not popular to raise these questions—especially when Bath Iron Works is the largest industrial employer in the state.

Soon after George W. Bush became president, he pulled the United States out of the 1972 Anti-Ballistic Missile (ABM) Treaty that limited the deployment of missile defense systems that are key elements in Pentagon first-strike attack planning. This led to the eventual creation of the Missile Defense Agency, and today we see U.S. deployments of missile defense systems on the land and on board navy ships being used to surround Russia and China.

Each year the U.S. Space Command conducts a computer war game in which they practice a first-strike attack on Russia and China. They call it the blue team against the red team. In this war game the first weapon used to attack China is the successor to the space shuttle—the military space plane—that during testing has shown the ability to stay in orbit for a full year without a pilot on board. It's really a superdrone. In the computer war game the military space plane drops back toward Earth and hits China.

Other weapon systems under the direction of Strategic Command's "Prompt Global Strike" program are then unleashed.

When Russia and China attempt to fire their remaining nuclear forces, the "missile defense" systems are used to pick off that retaliatory strike, giving the Pentagon a "successful" first strike. Thus, missile defense—or we should call it missile offense—is the shield used after the U.S. first-strike sword is thrust into the heart of another nation.

Russia and China have said repeatedly that any hopes for real nuclear disarmament are out the door as long as the United States continues to test and deploy these missile offense systems. The systems are destabilizing and make the reality of launch-on-warning more of a problem than ever.

The modernization of nuclear weapons, now under way at Sandia National Laboratories and elsewhere, is creating dramatic new instabilities in U.S.-Russian nuclear affairs. What is billed in Washington as necessary "modernization" or "repair" is really a new arms race, conducted against a backdrop of expanding missile defense deployments.

Today the United States is deploying land- and sea-based missile defense systems (including radars) in Romania, Poland, and Turkey and on ships in the Black, Mediterranean, Baltic, Barents, and Bering Seas. These deployments are directly aimed at Russia (although the Pentagon claims they are intended for Iran).[1]

Coupled with the hyperaggressive NATO expansion up to the Russian border, these deployments have forced Moscow into a red-alert corner. Recently the U.S. Army's Second Cavalry Regiment, driving armored personnel carriers and other military vehicles, rolled through the streets of Narva, Estonia, just three hundred yards from the Russian border—a dramatic example of the insane Pentagon military confrontations that are being created in Eastern Europe. The United States is just poking Russia to get a response.

Imagine if the reverse were happening and Russia was deploying military forces in Canada or Mexico. We'd go ballistic!

The U.S. Navy recently sent a nuclear submarine into the Arctic with *New York Times* columnist Thomas Friedman along for the ride. In his column afterward, Friedman quoted Jonathan Greenert, chief of naval operations: "In our lifetime, what was [in effect] land and prohibitive to navigate or explore, is becoming an ocean, and we'd better understand it. We need to be sure that our sensors, weapons and people are proficient in this part of the world," so that we can "own the undersea domain and get anywhere there."[2] Just look at a map and note that Russia has the largest land border with the Arctic Ocean.

At the same time, these missile defense systems are being positioned in South Korea, Japan, Okinawa, Guam, Taiwan, and on Aegis destroyers throughout the Pacific Ocean. They are aimed at China, though similarly Washington claims they are in response to North Korea.[3]

Last October I organized a peace walk through Maine to help shine a light on our state's growing economic dependence on military spending. We began the walk up in the beautiful mountain and lakes region called Rangeley, where the Pentagon's Missile Defense Agency is considering putting up to sixty ground-based missile defense interceptors.

Narrow, winding roads would have to be bulldozed and widened, and huge holes would have to be blasted into the mountains in order to insert the missile silos. Toxic rocket fuel would be trucked in and stored—the same rocket fuel that is now contaminating water sources in twenty-two states across the nation. The whole plan would be an environmental disaster and would cost taxpayers more than $4 billion.[4]

We came to find out the Pentagon didn't want this expensive program, but pressure on Congress from the Boeing Company forced it to go forward with an environmental impact statement process and public hearings in four states (including Maine) to select a possible "East Coast deployment" site for a missile defense base.[5]

Another major weapons program being built that the Pentagon

did not actually want is also in Maine. General Dynamics Corporation owns Bath Iron Works, where destroyers for the navy are built. The standard Aegis destroyers cost $1.5 billion each and are outfitted with missile defense interceptor missiles, which have had much success in their testing program. But when Obama became president, he forced the navy to build the new high-tech "stealth" destroyer called the *Zumwalt*, the job of which is to sneak up on China and blast it with electromagnetic railguns and other weapons systems. This is part of Obama's "pivot" of 60 percent of U.S. military forces into the Asia-Pacific region to provocatively confront and control China.

The majority stockholders in General Dynamics are the Crown family of Chicago, who helped Obama get elected to the presidency. He owed them, and the new *Zumwalt*-class stealth destroyer, at a cost to taxpayers of between $4 billion and $6 billion per copy, is their reward.

As part of the U.S. pivot to China, the Pentagon needs more airfields for warplanes, barracks for troops, and ports of call for the warships being redeployed into the Asia-Pacific region. So in places like Jeju Island, South Korea, we see a five-hundred-year-old farming and fishing culture being torn apart, and a UNESCO World Heritage Site's soft coral reefs being destroyed as a naval base is being built for U.S. nuclear subs, aircraft carriers, and destroyers.

In the United States today, 54 percent of every federal discretionary tax dollar goes to the Pentagon to fund the cancerous war machine. Our communities have become addicted to military spending as our physical and social infrastructure continues to deteriorate. There is virtually no money for anything else these days as we witness austerity cuts in social programs all over the nation.

The Pentagon says that America's role under corporate globalization of the world economy will be "security export." We won't have conventional jobs making things useful to our communities; instead we will build weapons for endless war and send our kids overseas to die for corporate profit.

Today, the United States is the number one exporter of weapons in the world.[6] And when weapons are your number one industrial export product, what is your global marketing strategy for that product line? What does it say about the soul of our nation that we have to keep selling weapons and killing people in order to provide jobs so workers can feed their families?

The Pentagon has the largest carbon boot print on the planet, but, sadly, there is little acknowledgment of that fact by most climate change groups, which well illustrates the "off limits" nature of the growing military domination of our society.

We have become an occupied nation. The corporate oligarchy in Washington uses space-based technologies to spy on us and to direct all warfare on the planet. In a way, you could call today's expensive military satellites the "triggers" that make high-tech weapons like drones and offensive missiles work. These satellites allow the military to see everything, hear everything, and to target virtually every place on the planet. We are sold the line that high-tech robotic war will save American lives and will be a cheaper way to fight.

The military-industrial complex has become the primary resource-extraction service for corporate capitalism and is preparing future generations for a dead-end street of perpetual war. Due to the fiscal crisis across the nation, engineering, computer science, mathematics, astronomy, and chemistry departments in colleges and universities have become increasingly dependent on Pentagon funding.

In the United States, at the end of the Cold War, approximately 40 percent of all scientists, engineers, and technical professionals currently work in the military sector.[7] This is a colossal waste of talent and intellectual resources as we face the coming reality of climate change.

We have also begun to militarize space, in part as a way to practice resource extraction on planetary bodies. The Space Command's job will be to control the pathway on and off our planet. The aerospace industry says it needs nuclear power in space for mining the sky. Nuclear reactors on rockets will be needed to give them the capability to reach Mars. International space law is now being rewritten by corporate interests to allow their control of the planetary bodies. The industry plan is to scrap the United Nations Outer Space Treaty and Moon Agreement, giving corporate entities full access to private mining operations on celestial bodies. Privatization of space is the plan.

Rovers on Mars are currently powered with plutonium-238. I organized campaigns to oppose nuclear launches from the space center in Florida in 1989, 1990, and 1997. Future mining colonies on the planetary bodies would be nuclear powered, requiring launches of nuclear materials into space on rockets that history has proven are vulnerable to explosion.

Space entrepreneur Elon Musk says we must move our civilization to Mars. The Mars Society says the Earth "is a rotting, stinking, dying planet" and that we have to terraform Mars to make it habitable. Imagine how much money that would cost.

When the Civil War and the Indian Wars ended, the military-industrial complex at that time saw an end to its massive war profits. It needed an enemy to keep the military production lines humming. So a strategy was developed: Journalists and artists were paid to fabricate stories about Crazy Horse, the great Lakota warrior who had been brought onto the reservation in South Dakota in 1877. They reported he had broken out and gone back on the warpath, killing innocent white children, raping white women, and burning their houses to the ground. These stories were printed in major papers across the nation and the American people were afraid and outraged. Congress swung into action and appropriated more money for weapons production, while Crazy Horse and Sitting Bull sat inside their tepees on the reservation without a gun to their names.

Similarly, in our time, we've seen the military-industrial complex fabricate stories about "weapons of mass destruction" in Iraq, and today we see ISIS (which was trained, armed, and funded by the

CIA, Saudi Arabia, and Jordan) as the justification for the United States to get back into Iraq and bomb Syria. Putin has been demonized by the Western media, creating the false notion that he is on the warpath to re-create the Soviet Union.

Studies by the economics department at the University of Massachusetts–Amherst reveal that military spending creates the fewest jobs relative to spending on solar, rail, wind turbines, education, health care, repairing our water and sewer systems, and fixing our roads and bridges, each of which creates many more jobs with the same amount of money.[8]

Abolitionist Frederick Douglass reminded us that power concedes nothing without a demand. When it comes to our current economic system, called "militarism," we should be demanding its conversion and the jobs that would result from that transformation. Without massive cuts in the Pentagon budget, how can we ever kick our addiction to weapons and kick-start our needed social redirection?

The militarization of everything around us is a spiritual sickness. Lakota holy man Lame Deer talked about the green frog skin—the dollar bill—and how the white man was blinded by his love for the paper money. His spiritual connection to Mother Earth was broken. It is time to repair the sacred hoop.

The reallocation of funding from the military to the peace, environmental, labor, and social justice movements could be a transformative strategy that would unify our disparate efforts and provide the despondent American people with a positive vision for the future. We don't have time to waste.

5

The Plutonium Problem

Bob Alvarez

The Nuclear Non-Proliferation Review Conference (NPT Rev-Con) takes place at the United Nations headquarters every five years. The treaty was enacted in 1970, and currently 191 nations have joined it. In 1995 parties to the treaty agreed to its indefinite extension. To a large extent, the treaty was a product of consensus defined by international regimes during the Cold War.

The treaty has eleven articles that rest on three conceptual pillars.

- *Nonproliferation:* The five nuclear-weapon states (at that time when the treaty entered into force) agree not to transfer nuclear weapons or to help develop nuclear weapons in nonweapon states. Nonweapon states also agree to accept international safeguards.
- *Disarmament:* As embodied in Article VI, the five nuclear-weapon states—the United States, Soviet Union (now Russia), United Kingdom, France, and China—are to halt the nuclear arms race and undertake negotiations "in good faith" to achieve nuclear and general disarmament.
- *Peaceful Uses of Atomic Energy:* Nations can transfer nuclear technologies and materials to signers of the NPT, and these nations have "an alienable right" to develop civil uses of atomic energy.

The Plutonium Problem

Plutonium makes up about 1 percent of spent nuclear fuel and is a powerful nuclear explosive, requiring extraordinary safeguards and security to prevent theft and diversion. It took about six kilograms to fuel the atomic bomb that devastated Nagasaki in 1945. Unlike plutonium bound up in highly radioactive spent nuclear fuel, separated plutonium does not have a significant radiation barrier to prevent theft and bomb making, especially by terrorists.

Nuclear power involves dual-use technologies that can be used to develop nuclear weapons. In fact, the first major U.S. generator

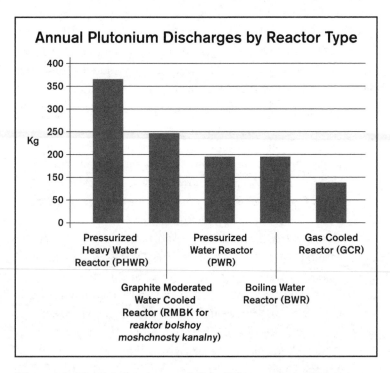

Figure 4.1. The global nuclear power fleet discharges nearly 100 metric tons of plutonium per year. About 20 percent of the nuclear power plants (77) are based on original designs for the production of plutonium for weapons.

of nuclear-power electricity in the 1960s was a dual-purpose reactor operating at the Hanford site producing plutonium for the U.S. nuclear weapons program.

One out of five power reactors in operation throughout the world currently is based on original designs to produce plutonium for nuclear weapons. In 2015 the International Atomic Energy Agency estimated that nuclear power plants generated 380,500 metric tons of spent nuclear fuel, which contain roughly 3,800 tons of plutonium.

The most efficient producer of plutonium is the pressurized heavy-water reactor (PHWR). This reactor runs on natural uranium that doesn't require enrichment, and is moderated with deuterium, also known as heavy water. It doesn't require shutdowns to discharge spent fuel, which makes it more difficult to safeguard because spent fuel rods are discharged out of the reactor while the reactor is still going. By comparison, light-water reactors require low-enriched uranium and have to be shut down for spent fuel discharging and refueling.

Data collected by the DOE's Idaho National Laboratory indicates PHWRs produce nearly twice as much plutonim-239 as light-water reactors. Designed at the University of Chicago during the Manhattan Project in World War II, five pressurized heavy-water reactors were deployed at the Savannah River Plant in South Carolina and became "workhorses" producing a large fraction of nuclear weapons material for the U.S. nuclear weapons program. They are deployed and sold by Canada as CANDU reactors (short for CANada Deuterium Uranium).[1] The PHWR has also become a major concern for nuclear proliferation. This type of reactor provided India and Israel with plutonium for their first nuclear weapons and is providing Pakistan with plutonium for its nuclear weapon. Iran is currently converting its PHWR to refrain from producing weapons-grade plutonium as part of the nuclear deal framework with the United States, permanent members of the UN Security Council, and the European Union.

Nuclear Recycling

Over the past few years, attention to the recycling of nuclear power spent fuel has grown. Fears of global warming due to fossil fuel burning have given nuclear energy a boost; over the next fifteen years dozens of new power reactors are planned worldwide. To promote nuclear energy, the Bush administration sought to establish international spent nuclear fuel recycling centers that are supposed to reduce wastes, recycle uranium, and convert nuclear explosive materials, such as plutonium, to less troublesome elements in advanced power reactors.

The key to recycling is being able to reuse materials while reducing pollution, saving money, and making the Earth a safer place. On all accounts, nuclear recycling fails the test.

In order to recycle uranium and plutonium in power plants, spent fuel has to be treated to chemically separate these elements from other highly radioactive by-products. As it chops and dissolves used fuel rods, a reprocessing plant releases about fifteen thousand times more radioactivity into the environment than nuclear power reactors and generates several dangerous waste streams.[2] If placed in a crowded area, a few grams of waste would deliver lethal radiation doses in a matter of seconds. The recycling plants also pose enduring threats to the human environment for tens of thousands of years.

European reprocessing has created higher risks and has spread radioactive waste across international borders. Radiation doses to people living near the Sellafield reprocessing facility in England were found to be ten times higher than for the general population.[3] Denmark, Norway, and Ireland have sought to close the French and English plants because of their radiological impacts.[4] Discharges of iodine 129, for example, a very long-lived carcinogen, have contaminated the shores of Denmark and Norway at levels a thousand times higher than nuclear weapons fallout.[5] Health studies indicate that significant excess childhood cancers have occurred near French and

English reprocessing plants.[6] Experts have not ruled out radiation as a possible cause, despite intense pressure from the nuclear industry to do so.[7]

Nuclear recycling in the United States has created one of the largest environmental legacies in the world. Between the 1940s and the late 1980s, the Department of Energy and its predecessors reprocessed tens of thousands of tons of spent fuel in order to reuse uranium and make plutonium for nuclear weapons.

By the end of the Cold War about 100 million gallons of high-level radioactive wastes were left in aging tanks that are larger than most state capitol domes. More than a third of some two hundred tanks have leaked and threaten water supplies such as the Columbia River.[8] The nation's experience with this mess should serve as a cautionary warning. According to the Department of Energy, treatment and disposal will cost more than $100 billion; and after twenty-six years of trying, the Energy Department has processed less than 1 percent of the radioactivity in these wastes for disposal.[9] By comparison, the amount of waste from spent power reactor fuel recycling in the United States would dwarf that of the nuclear weapons program—generating about twenty-five times more radioactivity.[10]

Since the 1970s, the United States has refrained from reprocessing commercial spent power reactor fuel to use plutonium in power plants. Instead, intact spent fuel rods are sent directly to a repository—a "once through" nuclear fuel cycle. Radioactive materials in spent fuel are bound up in ceramic pellets and are encased in durable metal cladding, planned for disposal deep underground in thick shielded casks.

Although the United States continued to reprocess spent fuel from military reactors, the "once through" fuel cycle was adopted by President Carter in 1977 for commercial nuclear power. Three years earlier, India had exploded a nuclear weapon using plutonium separated from power reactor spent fuel at a reprocessing facility. President Ford responded in 1976 by suspending reprocessing in the United States. President Carter converted the suspension into a ban, while issuing a strong international policy statement against establishing plutonium as fuel in global commerce. President Carter's decision reversed some twenty years of active promotion by the Department of Energy's predecessor, the U.S. Atomic Energy Commission, of the "closed" nuclear fuel cycle. The Commission had spent billions of dollars in an attempt to commercialize reprocessing technology to recycle uranium and provide plutonium fuel for use in "fast" nuclear power reactors.

Nuclear recycling advocates are seeking to overturn this longstanding policy and point to a new generation of "fast" reactors to break down plutonium so it can't be used in weapons. Since the 1940s, it was understood that "fast" reactors generate more subatomic particles, known as neutrons, than conventional power plants, and it is neutrons that split uranium atoms to produce energy in conventional reactors. The United States actively promoted plutonium-fueled fast reactors for decades because of the potential abundance of neutrons, declaring that they held the promise of producing electricity and making up to 30 percent more plutonium than they consumed.

With design changes, fast reactors are, ironically, being touted in the United States as a means to get rid of plutonium. However, the experience with "fast reactors" over the past fifty years is laced with failure. At least fifteen "fast" reactors have been closed due to costs and accidents in the United States, France, Germany, England, and Japan. There have been two fast reactor fuel meltdowns in the United States, including a mishap near Detroit in the 1960s. Russia operates the remaining fast reactor, but it has experienced fifteen serious fires in twenty-three years.[11]

Plutonium is currently used in a limited fashion in nuclear energy plants by being blended with uranium. Known as mixed oxide fuel (MOX), it can be recycled only once or twice in a commercial nuclear power plant because of the buildup of radioactive contaminants. According to a report to the French government in

2000, the use of plutonium in existing reactors doubles the cost of disposal.[12]

The unsuccessful history of fast reactors has created a plutonium legacy of major proportions. Of the 370 metric tons of plutonium extracted from power reactor spent fuel over the past several decades, about one-third has been used. Currently, about 200 tons of plutonium sits at reprocessing plants around the world—equivalent to the amount in some 30,000 nuclear weapons in global arsenals.[13]

The key to nuclear nonproliferation is not access to knowledge, it's access to the actual explosive materials. This is the essential safeguard that's required. The secrets of how to make nuclear weapons are not so secret anymore; and the technologies, while some are hard to come by, can be obtained. But it's access to the nuclear weapons materials, especially plutonium, enriched uranium, and uranium 233, that must be addressed.

As a senior energy advisor in the Clinton administration, I recall attending a briefing in 1996 by the National Academy of Sciences on the feasibility of recycling nuclear fuel. I'd been intrigued by the idea because of its promise to eliminate weapons-usable plutonium and to reduce the amount of waste that had to be buried, where it could conceivably seep into drinking water at some point in its multimillion-year-long half-life.

But then came the Academy's unequivocal conclusion: the idea was supremely impractical.[14] It would cost up to $500 billion in 1996 dollars and take 150 years to accomplish the transmutation of plutonium and other dangerous long-lived radioactive toxins. Ten years later the idea remained as costly and technologically unfeasible as it was in the 1990s. In 2007 the Academy once again tossed cold water on the Bush administration's effort to jump-start nuclear recycling by concluding that "there is no economic justification for going forward with this program at anything approaching a commercial scale."[15]

But after a period of several hundred years, when the fission products in spent nuclear fuel decay and greatly reduce the radiation barrier, a great deal of plutonium, in the thousands of metric tons, becomes much more accessible. What will we do with all this plutonium we've been generating worldwide? How can we even predict what the world will be like three hundred years from now? Figuring out how to geologically dispose of spent power reactor fuel without having to reprocess it, is a key long-term strategic problem, with no easy solution.

6

Nuclear Weapons and Artificial Intelligence

Max Tegmark

I. S.T.U.P.I.D.

Nearly 13.8 billion years after our Big Bang, about five hundred years after inventing the printing press, we humans decided to build a contraption called the Spectacular Thermonuclear Unpredictable Population Incineration Device, abbreviated STUPID. It's arguably the most costly device ever built on this beautiful spinning ball in space that we inhabit, but the cost hasn't prevented many people from saying that building and maintaining it was a good idea. This may seem odd, given that essentially nobody on our ball wants STUPID to ever get used.

It has only two knobs on the outside, labeled X and P, but despite this apparent simplicity, it's actually a very complicated device. It's a bit like a Rube Goldberg machine inside, so complex that not a single person on our planet understands how 100 percent of it works. Indeed, it was so complicated to build that it took the talents and resources of more than one country who worked really hard on it for many, many years. Many of the world's top physicists and engineers worked to invent and build the technology for doing what this device does: creating massive explosions around the planet. But that was only part of the effort that went into it: to overcome human inhibitions toward triggering the explosions, STUPID also involves state-of-the-art social engineering, putting people in special uniforms and using peer pressure and the latest social coercion techniques to make people do things they normally wouldn't do. Fake alerts are created where people who refuse to follow missile launch protocols are fired and replaced, and so on.

Let's now focus on how STUPID works. What are these two knobs? The X knob determines the total explosive power of the device. The P knob determines the probability that this thing will go off during any random year for whatever reason. As we'll see, one of the nifty features of it is that it can spontaneously go off even if nobody wants it to.

One can tune the settings of these two knobs, X and P. Let's look a bit at how the setting of these two dials has evolved over time. The X knob was set to zero until 1945, when we physicists figured out how to turn it up. We started below twenty kilotons with the Hiroshima and Nagasaki bombs, and by the time we got to the "Tsar Bomba" in 1961, we were up to fifty megatons—thousands of times more powerful. The number of bombs also grew dramatically, peaking at around 63,000 in the mid-1980s, dropping for a while, and then holding steady at around 16,000 hydrogen bombs in recent years, about 4,000 of which are on hair-trigger alert, meaning that they can be launched on a few minutes' notice.[1] Although those who decided to build STUPID argued that they had considered all factors and had everything under control, it eventually emerged that they had missed at least three crucial details.

II. Nuclear Winter

First, radiation risks had been underestimated, and over $2 billion in compensation has been paid out to victims of radiation exposure from uranium handling and nuclear tests in the United States alone.[2] Second, it was discovered that using STUPID had the potential of causing a nuclear winter, which wasn't realized until about four decades after STUPID's inauguration—oops! Regardless of whose cities burned, massive amounts of smoke reaching the upper troposphere would spread around the globe, blocking out enough sunlight to transform summers into winters, much like when an asteroid or supervolcano caused a mass extinction in the past. When the alarm was sounded by both U.S. and Soviet scientists in the 1980s, this contributed to the decision of Ronald Reagan and Mikhail Gorbachev to start turning down the X knob.[3]

Today's climate models are significantly better than those run on the supercomputers of the 1980s, whose computational power was inferior to that of your smartphone. This enables more accurate nuclear winter forecasts.

This calculation used a state-of-the-art general circulation model from NASA, which includes a module to calculate the transport and removal of aerosol particles, as well as a full ocean general circulation model with calculated sea ice, thus allowing the ocean to respond quickly at the surface and on yearly timescales in the deeper ocean.[4] This was the first time that an atmosphere-ocean general circulation model was used in this context, and the first time that the time horizon was extended to a full decade. Unfortunately, the increased accuracy has revealed gloomier findings: cooling by about 20°C (36°F) in much of the core farming regions of the United States, Europe, Russia, and China (by 35°C in parts of Russia) for the first two summers, and about half that even a full decade later.[5]

What does that mean in plain English? One doesn't need much farming experience to conclude that near-freezing summer temperatures for years would eliminate most of our food production. It's hard to predict exactly what would happen after thousands of Earth's largest cities are reduced to rubble and global infrastructure collapses, but whatever small fraction of all humans don't succumb to starvation, hypothermia, or disease would need to cope with roving armed gangs desperate for food.

Given the specter of nuclear winter, it has been argued that the traditional nuclear doctrine of Mutual Assured Destruction (MAD) has been replaced by Self-Assured Destruction (SAD): even if one of the two superpowers were able to launch its full nuclear arsenal against the other without any retaliation whatsoever, nuclear winter would assure its self-destruction.[6] Needless to say, there are many uncertainties in nuclear winter predictions—for example, in how much smoke is produced and how high up it gets, which determines its longevity. Given this uncertainty, there is absolutely no basis for arguing that the X knob is currently set low enough to guarantee the survival of most humans.

III. Accidental Nuclear War

Let's turn to the other knob, P: the probability that STUPID just goes kaboom for whatever reason. A third thing that the STUPID builders overlooked was that P is set to an irrationally large value. My own guess is that the most likely way we'll get a nuclear war going is by accident (which can also include people through various sorts of misunderstandings). We don't know what P is and estimates vary widely. However, we know for sure that it's not zero, since there have been large numbers of close calls caused by all sorts of things: computer malfunction, power failure, faulty intelligence, navigation error, bomber crash, satellite explosion, etc.[7] In fact, if it weren't for heroic acts of certain individuals—for example, Vasili Arkhipov and Stanislav Petrov—we might already have had a global nuclear war.

What about the change of P over time—how has P changed? Even though P certainly dropped after 1990, when tensions subsided between the United States and Russia, it might very well have gone up quite a bit again, and there are various reasons for this. The recent increase in mistrust and saber rattling between the United States and Russia obviously increases P, but there are also other seemingly unrelated developments that can potentially make P larger. As just one small example among many that have been discussed, the U.S. plan to replace two out of the twenty-four Trident submarine-launched ballistic missiles with conventional warheads, allegedly for potential use against North Korea, provides opportunities for misunderstanding. An adversary seeing this missile coming and considering a nuclear response would have no way of knowing what kind of warhead it has.

Let me end by talking about the impact of new technology on P, the risk of accidental nuclear war. Mutually Assured Destruction worked well when missiles were accurate enough to destroy a city but not accurate enough to destroy a silo. That made it very disadvantageous to launch any kind of first strike. Progress in computerized navigation has enabled much more precise targeting of missiles, reducing the disadvantage of a first strike, increasing P. Having accurate submarine-launched ballistic missiles near their targets also improves the prospects for a first strike. Most nuclear missile silos are within two thousand kilometer of an ocean, from which submarine-launched ballistic missiles can destroy them in seven to thirteen minutes depending on how "depressed" their trajectory is.[8] These shorter flight times give less time for the enemy to react, potentially making decision makers jumpier, and as a result, both the United States and Russia have now further increased P by placing thousands of missiles on alleged hair-trigger alert, ready to launch on warning before a single nuclear explosion has been confirmed.

What about artificial intelligence? There is broad consensus that artificial intelligence is now progressing rapidly. Although it is obviously very hard to forecast what will happen many decades from now, especially if AI turns out to surpass human cognitive abilities across the board, we can nonetheless draw some conclusions about likely developments in the near term as computers grow progressively more capable. For example, if we develop computer systems that are more reliable than people at properly following protocol, the military will have an almost irresistible temptation to implement them. We've already seen lots of the communications and command—and even analysis—be computerized in the military. Now, properly following proper protocol might sound like a pretty good thing, until you read about the Stanislav Petrov incident. Why was it that, in 1983 when he got this alarm that the United States was attacking the Soviet Union, Petrov decided not to pass it along to his superiors? Why did he decide not to follow proper protocol? Because he was human. If he had been a computer, he would have followed proper protocol, and some analysts speculate that a nuclear war might have started.

Another concern is that the more we computerize decision making, the more we take what Daniel Kahneman calls "system 1" out of the loop, and the more likely we are to lose valuable inhibitions and do dumb things.[9] Suppose that President Putin had a person with him with whom he was friends, who carried the nuclear launch codes surgically implanted next to her heart. If the only way for him to get them was to first stab her to death, this might make him think twice before starting a nuclear war and jeopardizing billions of lives. If instead all he needs to do is press a button, there are fewer inhibitions. If you have a superadvanced artificial intelligence system that the president just delegates the decision to, the inhibitions are even weaker, because he's not actually authorizing launch: he's just delegating his authority to this system, deciding that if something happens in the future, then please go ahead and follow proper protocol. Given our poor human track record of planning for the unforeseen (as illustrated in Stanley Kubrick's dark movie classic *Dr. Strangelove*), I think that this would increase P.

Then there are good old bugs. Has your computer ever given you the blue screen of death? Let's hope that the blue screen of death never turns into the red sky of death. Although it may be funny if it's just your unsaved work that got destroyed, it's less funny if it's your planet.

Finally, another current trend seems to be that as AI systems get more and more advanced, they become more and more inscrutable black boxes where we just don't understand what reasoning they use—but we still trust them. The GPS in our car recently instructed me to drive down a remote forest road that ended in an enormous snowbank. I have no idea how it came to that conclusion, but I trusted it. If we have a superadvanced computer system that is telling the Russian military and political leadership that yes, there is an American missile attack happening right now, and here's the cool map with high resolution graphics showing the missiles, they might just trust it without knowing how it came to that conclusion. If the system involved a human, they could ask it how it made that inference, and challenge its logic and input data, but if it was fully computerized, it might be harder to clear up misunderstandings before it was too late.

In summary, we don't know for sure that AI is going to increase the risk of accidental nuclear war, but we certainly can't say with confidence that it won't, and it's very likely that the effects will be significant one way or the other. So it would be naïve to think that the rise of artificial intelligence is going to have no impact on P.

IV. Outlook

Let me conclude by considering our place in a cosmic perspective. Something remarkable has happened 13.8 billion years after our Big Bang: life has evolved and our universe has become aware of itself. This life has done many fantastic things that are truly inspiring. We've created great literature, music, and film, and by using our curious minds we've been able to figure out more and more about our cosmos: how old it is, how grand it is, and how beautiful it is. Through this understanding, we've also come to discover technologies that enable us to take more control and actually start shaping our destiny, giving us the opportunity to make life flourish far beyond what our ancestors had dreamt of. But we've also done some extremely dumb things here in our universe, such as building STUPID and leaving it running with its current knob settings. We don't yet know what effect AI and other future developments will have on the P knob, but we can't rule out that things will get even worse.

We professors are often forced to hand out grades, and if I were teaching Risk Management 101 and had to give us humans a midterm grade based on our existential risk management so far, you could argue that I should give a B– on the grounds that we're muddling along and still haven't dropped the course. From my cosmological perspective, however, I find our performance pathetic, and can't give more than a D: the long-term potential for life is literally astronomical, yet we humans are jeopardizing this future with STUPID, and devote such a tiny fraction of our attention to reducing X and P that this doesn't even become the leading election issue in any country.

Why a D? Why not at least a B–, given that we're still not extinct? Many people view things from the traditional perspective that humans are the pinnacle of evolution, that life is limited to this planet, and that our focus should be limited to the next century or even just the next election cycle. In this perspective, wiping ourselves out within a century may not seem like such a big deal.

From a cosmic perspective, however, that would be utterly moronic. It would be completely naïve in a cosmic perspective to think that this is as good as it can possibly get. We have 1,057 times more volume at our disposal. We don't have just another century, but billions of years available for life to flourish. We have an incredible future opportunity that we stand to squander if we go extinct or in other ways screw up. People argue passionately about what the probability is that we wipe out in any given year: some guess it's 1 percent, some guess much lower probabilities such as 0.0001, some guess higher. Any of these numbers are just plain pathetic. If it's 1 percent we'd expect to last on the order of a century, which is pretty far from the billions of years of potential that we have. Come on, let's be a little more ambitious here!

If you still have doubts about whether our priorities are faulty, ask yourself who is more famous: Vasili Arkhipov or Justin Bieber? Then ask yourself which one of these two people we should thank for us all being alive today, because his courageous actions may have singlehandedly stopped a Soviet nuclear attack during the Cuban Missile Crisis.

The long-term survival of intelligent life on our planet is way too important to be left to leaders who have chosen to build and maintain STUPID. Fortunately, history holds many examples of how a small number of idealistic individuals can make a large difference for the better. For example, according to both Reagan and Gorbachev, a major contributing factor to the deep nuclear cuts that they began in the 1980s was the research of that handful of scientists who discovered nuclear winter. There are many worthwhile efforts around the globe aimed at turning down X and/or P. What can you personally do today to reduce the risk of nuclear apocalypse? Let me conclude by giving a concrete suggestion. I think that a strong and simple argument can be made that for any single country to have more than two hundred nuclear weapons is unethical:

1. Further increases in number cause negligible increases in deterrence: the deterrent effect on a potential attacker is already about as high as it can possibly get (please make a list of your two hundred largest cities and imagine them suddenly obliterated), and when deployed on submarine-launched ballistic missiles, they are virtually immune to a surprise first strike.

2. This is already at or above the threshold for causing a catastrophic global nuclear cold spell, so increasing the number merely jeopardizes the future of humanity for no good reason.[10]

If you accept this argument, then the logical conclusion is to stigmatize all efforts to replace or modernize nuclear weapons and any people or corporations that do so. The success in reducing smoking is an example to emulate. Why has the fraction of smokers in the United States plummeted from 45 percent in the 1950s to below 18 percent today, most of whom say they would like to quit? Smoking hasn't been banned, but it has been stigmatized. In the 1950s, smoking was the cool thing to do, and movie stars and TV anchors all did it, whereas today's hip, rich, and educated smoke much less than society's least fortunate members. After scientists finally won the debate about whether smoking was harmful, the growing stigma caused ever more powerful organizations to work against it. Replacing or modernizing nuclear weapons is clearly worse for humanity than smoking, so ask yourself what you can do to dissuade companies from investing in it. For example, the nonprofit organization "Don't Bank on the Bomb" provides all the information that you need to call your pension fund and encourage them to adopt a policy of not investing in nuclear weapons.[11] If they ask you why, you can say, "I know that building nuclear weapons isn't illegal, but I don't want my money invested in it, just as I don't want it invested in tobacco, gambling, or pornography." Many large banks, insurance companies, and pension funds have already adopted such nuclear-free investment policies, and the momentum is growing. If quadruple-digit nuclear arsenals get the stigma they deserve and eventually become downsized, this of course won't eliminate the threat of nuclear war, but it will be a huge first step in the right direction.

I am the president of the Future of Life Institute, a nonprofit organization we founded to help make humanity better stewards of this incredible opportunity we have to make life flourish for billions of years.[12] All of us founders love technology: every way in which 2015 is better than the Stone Age is because of technology. But we need to learn to handle technology wisely, and STUPID isn't wise—as Einstein put it: "The splitting of the atom has changed everything except the way we think. Thus we drift towards unparalleled catastrophe." When we invented fire, we messed up repeatedly, then invented the fire extinguisher. With more powerful technologies such as nuclear weapons, synthetic biology, and strong artificial intelligence, we should instead plan ahead and aim to get things right the first time, because it may be the only chance we'll get.

I'm an optimist and believe that we often underestimate both what we can do in our personal lives and what life and intelligence can accomplish in our universe. This means that the brief history of intelligence so far is not the end of the story, but just the beginning of what I hope will be billions of years of life flourishing in the cosmos. Our future is a race between the growing power of our technology and the wisdom with which we use it. Let's make sure that wisdom wins!

7

Weapons Scientists Up Close

Hugh Gusterson

In 1987 I moved to the small town of Livermore, California, home to one of the two main nuclear weapons laboratories in the United States. I was a graduate student in anthropology who had abandoned plans to do fieldwork in Africa for a more "relevant" topic—understanding what kinds of people chose to work on nuclear weapons, and why. I came to this project, to the trepidation of some faculty in my department, as someone who had been active in the Nuclear Weapons Freeze Campaign of the early 1980s.

My initial fieldwork in Livermore lasted from 1987 to 1989 and established my strange relationship to weapons scientists as, simultaneously, friends and objects of study. During those two years I moved three times, always sharing housing with someone who worked at the Lawrence Livermore National Laboratory. I joined a singles group, a baseball team, and a basketball team attached to the laboratory. I spent my Sunday mornings at different churches in town as a way of getting to meet lab employees (and was even invited to preach a sermon at the Unitarian Church). I spent many evenings at the Livermore Saloon and Casino, where the anthropologist writing his field notes over a beer while sitting at the bar was an object of some curiosity. Above all, I investigated the cultural world of the laboratory by asking each weapons scientist I met to introduce me to colleagues, then visiting these scientists in their homes to collect their life histories and explore with them the meaning of their work as weapons scientists. I ended up doing formal interviews with sixty-four employees of the laboratory as well as a number of local ministers, reporters, city officials, and spouses (actually, often, ex-spouses) of weapons scientists. Ultimately, I wrote two books about the scientists: *Nuclear Rites* and *People of the Bomb*.

Although this initial intense period of fieldwork ended in 1989, I have never really withdrawn from the weapons scientists' lives. I returned to Livermore for much of 1994–95, and I have spent many summers either back at Livermore or in Santa Fe, near the other nuclear weapons laboratory at Los Alamos, seeking to understand the ways the two weapons labs have adapted to the end of the Cold War and to the most devastating twist in their history in recent decades—the end of nuclear testing in 1992. I follow the weapons labs in the media and exchange e-mails and occasional phone calls with people I have come to know in Livermore and Los Alamos. And, whenever I publish something about the labs, I brace for the e-mails that inevitably follow. Sometimes they are appreciative and sometimes they are not.

When I first arrived in Livermore, I found that nuclear weapons scientists often had quite mistaken stereotypes of antinuclear activists. By the time I left Livermore, two years later, I realized that antinuclear activists often had misleading preconceptions about nuclear weapons scientists as well.

Weapons scientists had decided opinions about antinuclear activists, especially in the wake of the nuclear freeze movement and big protests at the laboratory in 1982 and 1983, which mobilized thousands of antinuclear activists, many of whom committed civil disobedience. Many weapons scientists assumed that activists were unemployed—how else would they be able to spend the day protesting?—and quite a few suggested that they were communists, or were in the pay of the Soviet Union. It was largely taken for granted at the lab that protestors were ill-informed about nuclear weapons. In fact, as I knew from my time in the nuclear freeze movement and from interviews I was doing with antinuclear activists in a parallel research endeavor, most protestors were middle-class people with university degrees and jobs. They may not, in most cases, have been experts on arms control, but many had taken time to educate themselves by attending lectures and reading books and pamphlets on the arms race. They often had overcrowded lives, devoting what spare time was left after work and family commitments to activism, and taking time off work to attend protests. (Maybe the most "respectable" protestor was a Methodist bishop who saw civil disobedience at the laboratory gates, for which she was arrested, as a vocational obligation.) The overwhelming majority were just as critical of the Soviet Union as of the United States, feeling that their lives were endangered equally by the policies of both superpowers. When I worked with the Nuclear Weapons Freeze Campaign in San Francisco, in 1984, we got a surprise office visit from the political attaché of the Soviet consulate, bringing us comradely greetings. He did not get a friendly reception.

But if antinuclear activists were victims of hostile stereotyping by weapons scientists, the reverse was also true. Many antinuclear activists assumed that weapons scientists were all politically conservative and that they did not think at all about the ethics of their work. After all, if they thought about ethics, how could they work on weapons of mass destruction? But, although it may be attractive to think of nuclear weapons scientists as ethically challenged right-wing ideologues, the truth is more interesting and more complicated.

To be sure, I did meet nuclear weapons scientists who voted Republican and, along with Ronald Reagan, saw the Soviet Union as an "evil empire." But I was surprised by how many weapons scientists were liberals who had donated time and money on behalf of progressive causes. (In retrospect, I should not have been so surprised given the FBI's alarm at the number of scientists who were communist fellow travelers and radicals in the original bomb project at wartime Los Alamos.) Thus I met weapons scientists who actively supported women's rights, gay rights, gun control, and environmental causes. I interviewed a weapons scientist who had risked his body as a freedom rider in the civil rights movement in the south. And I interviewed another weapons scientist, now a senior manager at Livermore, who had been very active in protests against the Vietnam War on his university campus. Lab scientists formed the backbone of the local antigrowth campaign that successfully reserved large swaths of open space in Livermore as off-limits to local developers who sought to cram generic subdivisions into every nook and cranny of open space. According to the informal straw poll I took among lab employees in 1988, more supported Michael Dukakis than Ronald Reagan in the presidential election.

So why did such people—about two-thirds of them active churchgoers—want to make nuclear weapons their life's work? Some did give ideological reasons—most notably an older man who referred repeatedly to his "monolithic anticommunism" as a reason for coming to Livermore in the 1950s—but most spoke more about Livermore as an attractive environment for doing scientific research. They appreciated the lab's reputation for excellence, the state-of-the-art supercomputer and laser technology the lab offered its researchers, and the emphasis on teamwork. One physics professor at an elite university commented privately to me on the irony that his most aggressive "alpha male" graduate students tended to become professors, while the "kinder, gentler" students with less-sharp elbows were more likely to go to the weapons labs where they would not have to constantly compete for funding and students.

Scientists were also drawn to the weapons labs by strong salaries. A recent article about Los Alamos, for example, reveals that the average salary there is over $100,000 a year, and Los Alamos County consistently places in the top five wealthiest counties in the country.[1] However, if wealth was their primary objective, many Livermore scientists could have earned more in the private sector and, when I asked them to reconstruct for me their decision to come to Livermore, most talked primarily about a well-resourced workplace that tackled exciting scientific challenges collegially.

Weapons scientists grew comfortable with this career choice in a context where they believed that nuclear weapons would not be used. What I call the central axiom of laboratory scientists is that nuclear weapons in the hands of advanced nations are a stabilizing force in the world that has prevented a third world war and kept the United States safe. While antinuclear activists see nuclear weapons as a genocidal threat looming over humankind, many weapons scientists told me they felt proud to have worked on weapons that had surely saved millions of lives by preventing World War III. One scientist, turning upside down the way antiwar activists look at the world, told me that he felt morally comfortable working on nuclear weapons, because they would never be used, but could not imagine working on, say, a conventional cruise missile or a land mine that would be used to kill people. When I asked weapons scientists if they could imagine a situation in which they would endorse using a nuclear weapon, quite a few said they could not. They said that if the United States was under nuclear attack, then the weapons they had designed would already have failed and it would be pointless to use them against others.

If we want to understand what makes it possible for scientists to work together on nuclear weapons, and to feel satisfaction in doing so, it is their shared commitment to this central axiom that nuclear deterrence really works, not a shared party political orientation and not a zombielike mass refusal to consider the ethics of their vocation. In fact, when I asked nuclear weapons scientists about the ethics of their work, I often got lengthy and forceful responses. I was told that if a democratically elected government has decided to stockpile nuclear weapons, it is ethical to give one's fellow citizens what they have voted for; that in a world where other countries have nuclear weapons, it would be unethical to leave one's own country undefended; that the weapons already exist and it might be an ethical obligation for those with the requisite skills to try to make them less likely to detonate by accident; and that weapons scientists are like designers of automobiles, who are not the ones responsible if drunk drivers get into accidents. Above all, I was told that the weapons were not classic weapons because they existed to deter war, not to fight it, and that the prevention of war was surely an ethical imperative. I did note that many scientists told me that they thought about the ethics of their work while their colleagues did not, so it was clear that much of this ethical thinking was being done alone.

For critics of nuclear weapons interested in entering into dialogue with weapons scientists with a view to changing their minds, it is surely more profitable to engage with the scientists' own central axiom than it is to accuse them of ethical blindness. Quite apart from the fact that the ethical accusation does not take full account of the fact that weapons scientists do have ethical arguments in support of their work, accusing one's political opponents of a lack of ethics, or of being in a state of denial, while undoubtedly a source of solidarity for the accusers, is inherently polarizing. Furthermore, recent revelations by the journalists Eric Schlosser, who recounts how a routine maintenance accident almost caused a hydrogen bomb to explode in Arkansas, and David Hoffman, who reveals a formerly unknown automated launch system in the former Soviet Union, surely invite everyone, pro- and antinuclear alike, to reconsider the safety of nuclear deterrence as it has been practiced, as does the chilling revelation in the documentary film *The Man Who Saved the World* that a handful of Soviet weapons control officers came within a hair's breadth of launching a nuclear attack on the United States in 1983 when their new early warning system generated a false alert that several American nuclear missiles were hurtling toward Soviet targets.[2] Such revelations change our empirical understanding of the risks and benefits of nuclear weapons and surely put a new onus on those who foresee indefinite reliance on nuclear weapons for our safety to defend that vision.

I arrived at Livermore at a particular moment in time—just as the Cold War and the era of nuclear testing was drawing to a close. For one to better understand the place of nuclear weapons scientists in the world, and their understanding of it, it will help to sketch out how the world of nuclear weapons scientists has changed over sixty years. Adapting a schema put forward by the anthropologist Joseph Masco, who writes about Los Alamos, I divide those sixty years into three periods, which I call the era of onrush, the era of normalization, and the era of simulation.

The Era of Onrush, 1945–62

The United States initiated the nuclear age when it tested an atomic bomb, designed at Los Alamos, in July 1945, and dropped two atomic bombs on the Japanese cities of Hiroshima and Nagasaki in August 1945. In 1949 the Soviet Union tested its own atomic bomb and an all-out nuclear arms race ensued. By 1952, thanks to the energetic advocacy of Edward Teller, the United States had established a second nuclear weapons laboratory in Livermore, and by 1955 the Soviets had a second nuclear weapons laboratory of their own at Chelyabinsk-70. In these years the pace of nuclear testing accelerated, climaxing in 1962 when the United States conducted almost one hundred nuclear tests and the Soviet Union seventy-eight. By that year the United States had accumulated an inventory of over 27,000 nuclear weapons while the Soviets had about 3,300.

This arms race was qualitative as well as quantitative, and it was in these years that the two superpower communities of weapons scientists had their great technical breakthroughs. They devised two different kinds of atomic bombs, one powered by the fissioning of uranium and the other by the fissioning of plutonium. They discovered how to use atomic bombs as triggers within hydrogen bombs that harnessed processes of nuclear fusion to generate much larger explosions. They also invented "boosted" weapons that, by means of capsules of tritium, used fusion processes to "boost" the yield of atomic bombs. And they figured out how to shrink nuclear weapons so they would fit atop intercontinental missiles that could traverse the globe in less than half an hour. These breakthroughs were achieved by some of the great names in the pantheon of nuclear weapons design. On the American side they included such figures as Robert Oppenheimer, Edward Teller, Stan Ulam, Ted Taylor, Richard Garwin, Hans Bethe, Seth Neddermeyer, Herb York, and Seymour Sack.

These technical developments took place within a framework of unrestrained competition with the Soviets. Except for a brief informal moratorium on nuclear testing at the end of the 1950s, there were no arms control treaties constraining the arms race between the superpowers. In the early 1950s General Curtis LeMay was urging a preemptive attack on the Soviet Union, and nuclear war felt like a real possibility. As the U.S. government made citizens rehearse "duck and cover" routines, some weapons scientists built bomb shelters in anticipation of the worst. (One of the three homes in which I lived in Livermore, which had formerly belonged to the legendary weapons scientist Stirling Colgate, had a bomb shelter that, by the late 1980s, had been converted into a wine cellar. And a retired laboratory manager I interviewed told me about the bomb shelter he built with several other families, and about their extensive debates over whether or not to shoot intruders who had not contributed toward the shelter but tried to enter it in the event of a nuclear attack.)

Many scientists had a vivid sense of what a nuclear war would be like because they had personally witnessed explosions of nuclear bombs that were tested either at the Nevada Test Site or, if they were larger hydrogen bombs, in the Pacific. Here is a description of one of those tests given to me by an old-timer from Livermore (who, admittedly, is not typical, since he eventually decided he could no longer work on such weapons). The test he described was, at "a few kilotons," quite small:

> There is this incredible flash of light, and you always
> go back to thinking how Oppenheimer describes this

incredible flash of light. He described it as brighter than
a thousand suns. Just incredibly intense. And it's very
frightening. Just terrifying. Just absolutely terrifying. I
was crouched over. I'm sure that I urinated in my pants
at the time as a result . . . And then while you're watch-
ing you see the difference in the index of refraction. You
could actually see the shock wave traveling toward you.
You know, there's a difference in the index of refraction.
And so you prepare to keep yourself from being blown
over by this blast, because it's a phenomenon. You just
see this thing coming, and it just takes forever to come,
and so you're sort of crouched, and finally the thing gets
to you, and the wind whips past you, and there's a lot of
dust and, yeah, your heart's beating a lot faster and you
just, you never forget it.

This first era in nuclear weapons science drew to a close with the
Cuban Missile Crisis of 1962. In the midst of that crisis President
John F. Kennedy privately estimated the odds of nuclear war between
the superpowers as one in three. Such a close brush with Armageddon induced the two superpowers to channel and constrain—but
not end—their nuclear competition in significant ways.

The Era of Normalization, 1963—91

In the last three decades of the Cold War the two superpowers
negotiated a set of arms control treaties that regulated and chan-
neled their nuclear rivalry while also normalizing it. These treaties stabilized deterrence, turning the arms race into an institu-
tionalized competition that was as much symbolic as it was a race
for actual military supremacy. These treaties included the SALT
I and SALT II treaties, elaborate texts that limited the numbers
of weapons the two nations could deploy in various categories.
They also included the ABM Treaty of 1972, which foreclosed the

possibility of a destabilizing race in antimissile technology, and the INF Treaty of 1987, which banned all intermediate-range nuclear missiles. If such treaties provided reassurance to weapons scientists that the arms race was not dangerously out of control, they did not much affect the laboratories' livelihood: once the laboratories had designed and tested a weapon, the mass production of the weapon was passed on to other facilities, and it made little difference to Livermore and Los Alamos whether fifty or five hundred copies of the weapon were made.

What did matter to the weapons laboratories were restraints on nuclear testing—their bread and butter. In 1963, and then again in the late 1970s, American and Soviet negotiators discussed a complete ban on nuclear testing. In 1963 negotiators could not agree on an inspection regime for a test ban, and so they settled for the more modest Limited Test Ban Treaty, which banned testing aboveground. (This treaty, negotiated in the aftermath of the Cuban Missile Crisis, was partly a response to the protests of the late 1950s against the public health risk posed by radiation from atmospheric nuclear testing.) In 1974, the Partial Test Ban Treaty limited the permissible size of underground tests to 150 kilotons. By the late 1970s Jimmy Carter and Leonid Brezhnev were again discussing a complete ban on nuclear testing. Harold Agnew, the director of Los Alamos at the time, has claimed that he talked Jimmy Carter out of such a ban during a meeting at the White House.[3]

In this era (toward the end of which I arrived to do my initial fieldwork) weapons design became routinized. The major design breakthroughs—the development of fusion and boosting and the miniaturization of warheads—lay in the past, and weapons designers were simply refining existing designs to improve their efficiency and safety. They were squeezing higher yields out of weapons with less plutonium, making the weapons a little lighter and smaller, developing designs that were less likely to detonate by accident, and substituting less toxic materials into the weapons. One university physicist who had a clearance and tracked the weapons labs told me that weapons design in these years required little in the way of brilliance. Showing a disdain for weapons science that was not uncommon among university physicists, he scoffed that it was like "polishing turds."

Meanwhile the force of the weapons, now tested underground, had become more difficult for their designers to grasp. Here is an account of an underground test at the Nevada Test Site described for me by the bomb's lead designer:

> And everything went smooth, and it went off and they show a picture on the TV screens there of a helicopter hovering above the site and you could actually see dust rising. I mean it's not like you're watching the old atmospheric tests. I mean it's pretty benign really. You can see a shock wave ripple across the earth. It's a couple thousand feet under the ground. Nevertheless you see a ripple, and under the ground there's still a fireball and that material gets molten. . . . That leads to the formation of the crater at the top. And so you're not allowed out to the site until the crater is actually formed, and that can happen in 30 seconds, it can happen in 10 hours. Turned out with mine that it happened in about an hour, and so then we could drive out to the site. And that was really awesome, standing there with this thing that was at least 100 yards across, and see what I had been looking at on my computer screen for years show up in this gigantic movement of the earth. It was as close as I've been to personal contact with what the force of the nuclear weapon is like, because I've never been present at an atmospheric burst, nor has anybody else in my generation. . . . And then some of the data starts to come in and by the end of the day it was clear that it was going to be a success. It was a very complicated shot, so I knew that would be good for my career.

This account illustrates the ways in which, by this time, nuclear testing had become normalized. The test is described in terms of a routinized set of rules and the designer compares his own test, and the crater it creates, with his colleagues'. He also notes the implications for his career. We might also note that the bomb's blast, experienced indirectly, is more abstract. The designer, who watches the test on TV, experiences the blast through signs of its displaced power: rising dust, a sinking crater, and scientific measurements. He sees no mushroom cloud, feels no heat, feels no blast. Instead, he struggles to grasp the relationship between the massive crater and calculations on his computer.

The Era of Simulation, 1992—?

The last U.S nuclear test was in 1992. After the Cold War ended and the Soviet Union fell apart, the U.S. government was faced with mounting opposition to nuclear testing both within the U.S. Congress and in the international community. Believing that there was little need to develop new nuclear weapons in the absence of a rival superpower, and concerned that the nonproliferation regime was in danger without a concession from the nuclear powers of the world to the nonnuclear powers, the George H.W. Bush administration agreed to a moratorium on nuclear testing, which became the basis for the Comprehensive Test Ban Treaty (CTBT) of 1996, signed by President Bill Clinton (but still not ratified). In the meantime, the number of U.S. nuclear weapons fell from a Cold War high of over thirty thousand to a little under five thousand warheads deployed or in active reserve today (with several thousand more awaiting dismantlement). The current number of Russian nuclear weapons, falling from a Cold War peak of around forty thousand, is roughly comparable. Under the New START Treaty of 2010, the two countries have agreed to reduce their deployed arsenals further, to 1,550 weapons each.

When the CTBT was signed in 1996, many antinuclear activists dismissed it as a meaningless gesture that would not stop nuclear weapons scientists from continuing to modernize nuclear weapons. But this is certainly not how the CTBT was seen within the weapons labs. The lab directors fought hard (and lost) to protect nuclear testing, even if this meant acquiescing to new restrictions on the permissible size or number of nuclear tests. The weapons labs were concerned that, in a world without nuclear testing, the U.S. stockpile would forever be confined to designs whose reliability had been demonstrated by testing, with only minor modifications possible. The evolution of the weapons scientists' dark art would be unnaturally frozen. They also wondered how disputes about the reliability of aging weapons would be resolved if, as a final resort, they could not test one to see if it worked. They worried that this was like asking a mechanic to certify that a car will work while forbidding turning the key in the ignition.

Laboratory managers also had other reasons for concern, grounded in the organizational culture of the labs. Traditionally, experienced designers had apprenticed novices by working with them on nuclear tests, and young designers were evaluated according to the skill they showed in designing components of test devices and, finally, in executing their own tests. The reader will recall that the weapons designer quoted earlier said that he felt relieved at the success of his nuclear test because it would be good for his career. Shorn of nuclear testing, the laboratories would have to find another way for older scientists to train their juniors and to evaluate their skill and judgment.

This other way was a program called "Science-Based Stockpile Stewardship," a lavishly funded ensemble of simulation technologies distributed across the laboratories. These technologies included: Livermore's $4.5 billion National Ignition Facility, the most powerful laser in the world, capable of transiently creating temperatures and pressures greater than those in the sun just a few hundred yards from a suburban housing estate; the Dual-Axis Radiographic Hydrotest Facility (DARHT) at Los Alamos, used to test the compression dynamics of atomic bombs from which the fissile material has been removed; the Z Machine at Sandia National Laboratories, an engineering laboratory supporting Livermore and Los Alamos, which uses magnetic fields to produce intense bursts of radiation; underground tests of small amounts of plutonium, at the Nevada Test Site, that stopped short of inducing a chain reaction; and supercomputers such as Livermore's Sequoia computer, which was the fastest in the world when it was unveiled in 2012.

The experimental facilities are used to simulate component processes within an exploding nuclear weapon. Scientists then use the results from these experiments to refine the supercomputer codes that model and predict the performance of a nuclear weapon. At Los Alamos the processes that make up a nuclear explosion can be turned into visual representations that are projected onto the walls of a facility called the CAVE (Cave Automatic Virtual Environment), and scientists can stand "inside" a nuclear explosion, magnifying and rewinding its component elements. If the first generation of weapons scientists witnessed firsthand the ferocious power of nuclear explosions and, in some cases, built themselves underground shelters—man-made caves if you like—in which to shelter from nuclear war, today's weapons designers have a more playful relationship to nuclear explosions, now sometimes rendered as psychedelia, and have designed a cave that allows them to step inside the explosion without harm.

Many weapons scientists have commented to me that, in the years of the Cold War, the pace of nuclear testing was such that new weapons were being designed and tested at breakneck speed, but the lab scientists were not allowed the time to probe the underlying science systematically. Although at some level knowledge and design are obviously connected, design was privileged over knowledge. In the era of simulation, the situation is reversed. Thanks to the stockpile stewardship program, weapons scientists have been able to refine their understanding of the physical processes underlying a nuclear explosion, but the design of the weapons themselves is broadly frozen. Anthropologist Joseph Masco writes that nuclear weapons scientists have become weapons gerontologists, seeking "to slow down time, to prevent nothing less than aging itself. . . . The arms race may be on hold in post–Cold War Los Alamos, but a new race against time is at the center of the Laboratory's nuclear mission, a programmatic effort to endlessly defer a future of aged, and perhaps derelict, U.S. nuclear machines." Weapons scientists worry about "the bomb itself as fragile body, exposed to the elements, aging, and increasingly infirm."[4]

I have tried to suggest here that nuclear weapons scientists have a set of beliefs about the meaning of their work, and that these beliefs have shifted over time in keeping with wider geopolitical changes. In the first nuclear era, up until the Cuban Missile Crisis, nuclear weapons scientists operated in a context where nuclear weapons had recently been used in war, thus conferring on them a degree of normalcy; two new superpowers, animated by mutually hostile global ideologies, each trying to push into the other's sphere, were competing without established rules of the road; one of those superpowers was, for part of this period, led by a dictator with the blood of millions of his own citizens on his hands; and the two superpowers' nuclear stockpiles, unregulated by arms control agreements, were growing rapidly in size and capability. It should hardly surprise us that an older generation of weapons scientists, living in the aftermath of the bloodletting of World War II, would have, in this context, seen the weapons they designed as the best means to hand for deterring the rival superpower, even though this posed the risk of nuclear war.

The generation of weapons scientists that followed after the Cuban Missile Crisis worked in a context where the arms race had become normalized in terms of both work practices and the matrix of treaties in the international system that regulated the nuclear competition. These scientists were doing a job as much as they were responding to an urgent call. The weapons were still designed to deter the Soviets, but the Soviets were now becoming a comfortable enemy. Whether they were right or not, it seemed to these scientists, much more than to those who had trained them, that the weapons were unlikely to be used.

The latest generation of scientists labors in a strangely liminal situation where the Russians hover between enemy and friend and the purpose of nuclear weapons is increasingly self-referential. Rather than existing to deter an actual enemy, the weapons exist because, in a world where the weapons exist, they must be deterred. They exist because the genie can't be put back in the bottle. The weapons are more about habit and less about mission. They exist because we cannot imagine a world without them, and yet we are no longer sure precisely what to do with them.

At the same time, in a way that I have characterized elsewhere as "orientalist," Americans are quite sure that the weapons are safe in *their* hands but not in the hands of those Third World countries that, it is presumed, will not know how to store them properly, or will not protect them from hotheaded military officers, or will be overtaken by religious fundamentalists. Apparently no revelations about our own history of near misses with nuclear disaster, no newspaper stories about fanatics and death cults within America's borders, can shake this sense of rationalist superiority. This dichotomy between advanced nations who can be trusted with nuclear weapons and Third World countries who cannot, legitimates the maintenance of the U.S. stockpile while anchoring the faith in rationality that undergirds the weapons scientists' conviction that our weapons will never be used.

For the youngest generation of weapons scientists this sense that nuclear weapons are benign in our rational hands is further enabled by the increasing abstraction of the weapons. Los Alamos director Harold Agnew said that "he would require every world leader to witness an atomic blast every five years while standing in his underwear 'so he feels the heat and understands just what he's screwing around with . . . because we're approaching an era where there aren't any of us left that have ever seen a megaton bomb go off. And once you've seen one, it's rather sobering.'"[5] Instead, we have moved to an opposite world where even the weapons designers are imaginatively estranged from the force they have brought forth. The destructive power that can destroy a city with an object the size of a grapefruit is now a cascade of numbers in a computer, a swirl of colors in the CAVE, a short black-and-white movie clip with a quaintly anachronistic soundtrack. And, as Agnew knew, there is a danger in this. Meanwhile the weapons themselves, these obdurate physical artifacts, age. The weapons scientists and the technicians periodically inspect them, open them up and replace parts they believe to be failing, perform upgrades, test the behavior of small samples of aging plutonium, fire up their lasers, and refine their supercomputer codes. And the weapons keep aging. So do the weapons scientists. Eventually there will be none left who have actually designed and tested a nuclear weapon. Weapons science will become increasingly like Latin in the university: a dead knowledge preserved by a priesthood poring over ancient texts. The weapons scientists themselves say that nuclear testing will never come back. They also say, with chagrin, that the weapons designs we are stuck with, the so-called "legacy designs," were designed to push yield-to-weight ratios to the limit and to be replaced within a couple of decades as the design production lines of the labs kept moving. They are temperamental nuclear Lamborghinis designed for extreme performance, not the dull Hondas you would want if long-term reliability were your priority.

One day—we do not know when, but the day will surely come—a group of weapons scientists will grow to doubt the reliability of one of the designs in the stockpile. What will happen then? Every year the lab directors write a letter to the president certifying the labs' continuing faith in the reliability of each weapons design. When President Bill Clinton signed the test ban treaty, he added a proviso that the United States reserved the right to resume testing if it lost technical confidence in its stockpile. Some activists worry that this makes us hostage to the weapons labs, giving them a private lever they can pull whenever they want to get testing back. Many weapons scientists have the opposite concern: they fear that the pressure not to resume testing would be so intense that the lab directors would continue to certify a design that was no longer deemed reliable by actual designers. But, in terms of the professional ethics of a scientist or engineer, keeping quiet while a superior asserts the reliability of an unreliable product is deeply problematic. Would they, some weapons scientists wonder, then have an obligation to step outside the chain of command, risking loss of their security clearance and even imprisonment, to share their concerns with members of Congress or with the media? Those scientists who told me many years ago that they thought it pointless to launch nuclear weapons if the United States were under nuclear attack might say that it does not matter if the weapons work; their only job is to deter. But they have many colleagues who will say that they cannot deter unless they are known to work.

But maybe nuclear weapons can be abolished before we reach this point. Most weapons scientists are skeptical that this would be politically feasible, or even desirable. Still, some years ago one highly regarded Livermore designer, now on the verge of retirement, told me that he had become a nuclear abolitionist. Wide-eyed, I asked how this could be possible. "Because a world without nuclear weapons is a world in which the U.S. would have uncontested military domination," he announced with a grin.

As always, be careful what you wish for.

8

What Would Happen If an 800-Kiloton Nuclear Warhead Detonated Above Midtown Manhattan?

Steven Starr, Lynn Eden, Theodore A. Postol

Russian intercontinental ballistic missiles are believed to carry a total of approximately one thousand strategic nuclear warheads that can hit the United States less than thirty minutes after being launched. Of this total, about 700 warheads are rated at 800 kilotons; that is, each has the explosive power of 800,000 tons of TNT. What follows is a description of the consequences of the detonation of a single such warhead over Midtown Manhattan, in the heart of New York City.

The Initial Fireball

The warhead would probably be detonated slightly more than a mile above the city, to maximize the damage created by its blast wave. Within a few tenths of millionths of a second after detonation, the center of the warhead would reach a temperature of roughly 200 million degrees Fahrenheit (about 100 million degrees Celsius), or about four to five times the temperature at the center of the sun.

A ball of superheated air would form, initially expanding outward at millions of miles per hour. It would act like a fast-moving piston on the surrounding air, compressing it at the edge of the fireball and creating a shock wave of vast size and power.

After one second, the fireball would be roughly a mile in diameter. It would have cooled from its initial temperature of many millions of degrees to about 16,000 degrees Fahrenheit, roughly 4,000 degrees hotter than the surface of the sun.

On a clear day with average weather conditions, the enormous

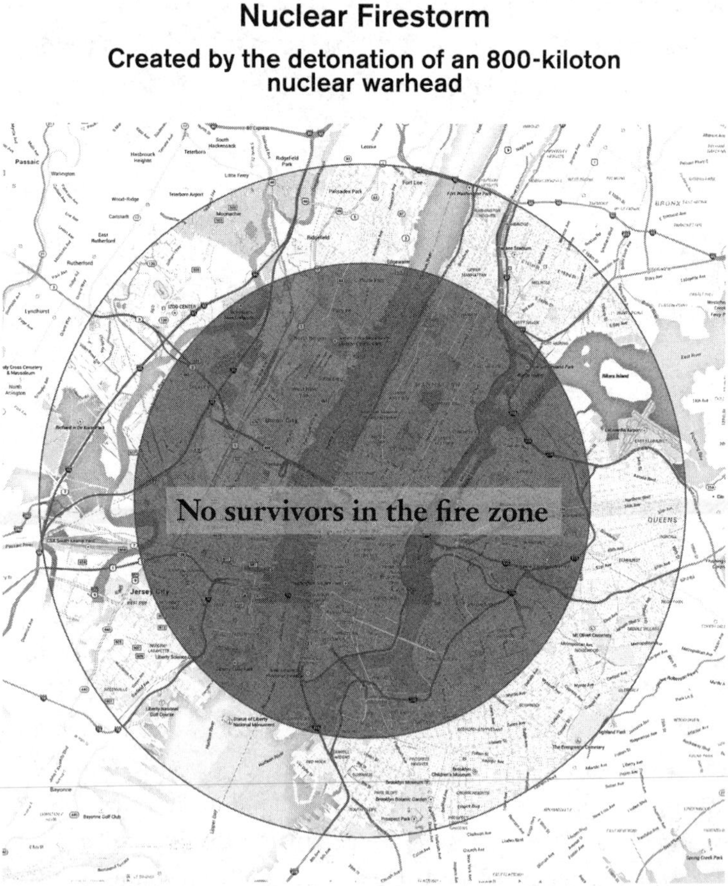
Nuclear Firestorm
Created by the detonation of an 800-kiloton nuclear warhead
No survivors in the fire zone
Passaic
QUEENS

Figure 8.1 Firestorm certain to occur in central grey zone, total area 90 square miles or 230 square kilometers. Firestorm likely to occur in the entire zone, total area 152 square miles or 389 square kilometers. Calculated for a clear day with average weather conditions. Map data: Google Imagery, 2015 Terrametrics.

heat and light from the fireball would almost instantly ignite fires over a total area of about 100 square miles.

Hurricane of Fire

Seconds after the detonation, fires set within a few miles of the fireball would burn violently. These fires would force gigantic masses of heated air to rise, drawing cooler air from surrounding areas toward the center of the fire zone from all directions.

As the massive winds drove flames into areas where fires had not yet fully developed, the fires set by the detonation would begin to merge. Within tens of minutes of the detonation, fires from near and far would join to form a single, gigantic fire. The energy released by this mass fire would be fifteen to fifty times greater than the energy produced by the nuclear detonation.

The mass fire, or firestorm, would quickly increase in intensity, heating enormous volumes of air that would rise at speeds approaching 300 miles per hour. This chimney effect would pull cool air from outside the fire zone toward the center of the fire at speeds of hundreds of miles per hour. These superheated ground winds of more-than-hurricane force would further intensify the fire. At the edge of the fire zone, the winds would be powerful enough to uproot trees three feet in diameter and suck people from outside the fire into it.

The inrushing winds would drive the flames from burning buildings horizontally along the ground, filling city streets with flames and firebrands, breaking in doors and windows, and causing the fire to jump, sometimes hundreds of feet, swallowing anything not already violently combusting.

These above-hurricane-force ground winds would have average air temperatures well above the boiling point of water. The targeted area would be transformed into a huge hurricane of fire, producing a lethal environment throughout the entire fire zone.

Ground Zero: Midtown Manhattan

The fireball would vaporize the structures directly below it and produce an immense blast wave and high-speed winds, crushing even heavily built concrete structures within a couple of miles of ground zero. The blast would tear apart high-rise buildings and expose their contents to the solar temperatures; it would spread fires by exposing ignitable surfaces, releasing flammable materials, and dispersing burning matter.

At the Empire State Building, Grand Central Station, the Chrysler Building, and St. Patrick's Cathedral, about one-half to three-quarters of a mile from ground zero, light from the fireball would melt asphalt in the streets, burn paint off walls, and melt metal surfaces within a half second of the detonation. Roughly one second later, the blast wave and 750-mile-per-hour winds would arrive, flattening buildings and tossing burning cars into the air like leaves in a windstorm. Throughout Midtown, the interiors of vehicles and buildings in the line of sight of the fireball would explode into flames.

Slightly more than a mile from ground zero are the neighborhoods of Chelsea, Murray Hill, and Lenox Hill, as well as the United Nations; at this distance, for a split second, the fireball would shine ten thousand times brighter than a desert sun at noon. All combustible materials illuminated by the fireball would spew fire and black smoke.

Grass, vegetation, and leaves on trees would burst into flames; the surface of the ground would explode into superheated dust. Any flammable material inside buildings (paper, curtains, upholstery) that was directly exposed to the fireball would also burst into flame. The surfaces of the bronze statues in front of the UN building would melt; marble surfaces exposed to the fireball would crack, pop, and possibly evaporate.

At this distance from the fireball, it would take about four seconds for the blast wave to arrive. As it passed over, the blast wave would engulf all structures and crush them; it would generate ferocious winds of 400 to 500 miles per hour that would persist for a few seconds.

The high winds would tear structural elements from buildings and cause them to disintegrate explosively into smaller pieces. Some of these pieces would become destructive projectiles, causing further damage. The superheated, dust-laden winds would be strong enough to overturn trucks and buses.

Two miles from ground zero, the Metropolitan Museum of Art, with all its magnificent historical treasures, would be obliterated. Two-and-a-half miles from ground zero, in Soho, the East Village, and Stuyvesant Town, the fireball would appear 2,700 times brighter than a desert sun at noon. There, thermal radiation would melt and warp aluminum surfaces, ignite the tires of autos, and turn exposed skin to charcoal, before the blast wave arrived and ripped apart the buildings.

Three to Nine Miles from Ground Zero

Midtown is bordered by the relatively wide Hudson and East Rivers, and fires would start simultaneously in large areas on both sides of these waterways (that is, in Queens and Brooklyn as well as Jersey City and West New York). Although the direction of the fiery winds in regions near the river would be modified by the water, the overall wind pattern from these huge neighboring fire zones would be similar to that of a single mass fire, with its center at Midtown, Manhattan.

Three miles from ground zero, in Union City, New Jersey, and Astoria, Queens, the fireball would be as bright as 1,900 suns and deliver more than five times the thermal energy deposited at the perimeter of the mass fire at Hiroshima. In Greenpoint, Brooklyn, and in the Civic Center of Lower Manhattan, clothes worn by people in the direct line of sight of the fireball would burst into flames or melt, and uncovered skin would be charred, causing third-degree and fourth-degree burns.

It would take twelve to fourteen seconds for the blast wave to travel three miles after the fireball's initial flash of light. At this distance, the blast wave would last for about three seconds and be accompanied by winds of 200 to 300 miles per hour. Low-rise and brownstone structures would be destroyed; high-rises would be at least heavily damaged.

Fires would rage everywhere within five miles of ground zero. At a distance of 5.35 miles from the detonation, the light flash from the fireball would deliver twice the thermal energy experienced at the edge of the mass fire at Hiroshima. In Jersey City and Cliffside Park, and in Woodside in Queens, on Governors Island and in Harlem, the light and heat to surfaces would approximate that created by six hundred desert suns at noon.

Wind speed at this distance would be 70 to 100 miles per hour. Buildings of heavy construction would suffer little structural damage, but all exterior windows would be shattered, and nonsupporting interior walls and doors would be severely damaged or blown down. Black smoke would effuse from wood houses as paint burned off surfaces and furnishings ignited.

Six to seven miles from ground zero, from Moonachie, New Jersey, to Crown Heights, Brooklyn, from Yankee Stadium to Corona, Queens, the fireball would appear three hundred times brighter than the desert sun at noon. Anyone in the direct light of the fireball would suffer third-degree burns to their exposed skin. The firestorm could engulf neighborhoods as far as seven miles away from ground zero, since these outlying areas would receive the same amount of heat as did the areas at the edge of the mass fire at Hiroshima.

Nine miles from ground zero, in Hackensack, Bayonne, and Englewood, New Jersey, as well as in Richmond Hill, Queens, and Flatlands, Brooklyn, the fireball would be about one hundred times brighter than the sun—bright enough to cause first- and second-degree burns to those in the line of sight. About thirty-six seconds after the fireball, the shock wave would arrive and knock out all the windows, along with many interior building walls and some doors.

No Survivors

Within tens of minutes, everything within approximately five to seven miles of Midtown Manhattan would be engulfed by a gigantic firestorm. The fire zone would cover a total area of 90 to 152 square miles (230 to 389 square kilometers). The firestorm would rage for three to six hours. Air temperatures in the fire zone would likely average 400 to 500 degrees Fahrenheit (200 to 260 degrees Celsius).

After the fire burned out, the street pavement would be so hot that even tracked vehicles could not pass over it for days. Buried, unburned material from collapsed buildings throughout the fire zone could burst into flames when exposed to air, months after the firestorm had ended.

Those who tried to escape through the streets would have been incinerated by the hurricane-force winds filled with firebrands and flames. Even those able to find shelter in the lower-level sub-basements of massive buildings would likely suffocate from fire-generated gases or be cooked alive as their shelters heated to oven-like conditions.

The fire would extinguish all life and destroy almost everything else. Tens of miles downwind of the area of immediate destruction, radioactive fallout would begin to arrive within a few hours of the detonation.

But that is another story.

PART TWO

TWENTY-FIRST-CENTURY NUCLEAR POLITICS

9

National Politics Versus National Security

Noam Chomsky

As we are all too well aware, in January, 2017, the Doomsday Clock was advanced to two-and-a-half minutes before midnight, a threat level that had not been reached for thirty years. The accompanying statement invoked the two major threats to survival: nuclear weapons and "unchecked climate change." The call condemned world leaders, who are endangering "every person on Earth [by] failing to perform their most important duty—ensuring and preserving the health and vitality of human civilization."[1]

This grim declaration naturally brought to mind another one issued just fifty years earlier: the appeal to the people of the world by Bertrand Russell and Albert Einstein, calling on them to face a choice that is "stark and dreadful and inescapable: Shall we put an end to the human race; or shall mankind renounce war?"—recognizing that war can quickly turn into terminal nuclear war.[2]

The Russell-Einstein appeal differs from the current declaration in two crucial respects. It did not include the threat of environmental catastrophe, then not sufficiently understood. And it directly addresses the people of the world, not the political leadership. The latter difference is of some importance. There is substantial evidence that on climate change, nuclear weapons planning, and international policies generally, the population seems in general more concerned than the political leadership.

It is hardly a secret that even the most free and democratic governments respond only in limited ways to popular will. For the United States, it is well established that a considerable majority of the population, at the lower end of the income/wealth scale, are effectively disenfranchised.[3] Influence increases slowly as one moves up the scale, and at the very top—a fraction of one percent—policy is pretty much determined. That being the case, the attitudes at the very top of the ladder are of great import. These are revealed dramatically in the poll of CEOs released in January 2015 at the Davos conference of "masters of the universe," as the business press describes them.[4]

The poll revealed that climate change did not merit inclusion among the top nineteen risks that concern CEOs. Worse still, at the top of their perceived risks was "overregulation"—that is, the prime method for addressing environmental catastrophe. Their overriding concern was growth prospects for their companies.

The result is not surprising. Whatever their individual beliefs, in their institutional roles the CEOs are constrained to adopt policies that are designed to "pose extraordinary and undeniable threats to the continued existence of humanity," in the words of the Doomsday Clock declaration. And given the CEOs' enormous role in determining state policy, it is no less surprising that policy lags behind public opinion on the concerns that have moved the Clock so close to midnight.

Much the same is true of attitudes toward international affairs. Popular opinion diverges significantly from that of the decision-making classes.[5] Among many other examples, a considerable majority have generally held that the UN, not the United States, should take the lead in international crises. Such views are so remote from elite opinion that they are barely even articulated publicly.

A good part of the reason is the nature of elite opinion. As often, it is the critical end of the spectrum that is the most informative. Here is an example from a featured article by the former director of the Carnegie Endowment for International Peace in the March 15,

2015, issue of the *New York Review of Books*, the leading U.S. intellectual journal, left-liberal in orientation: "American contributions to international security, global economic growth, freedom, and human well-being have been so self-evidently unique and have been so clearly directed to others' benefit that Americans have long believed that the U.S. amounts to a different kind of country. Where others push their national interests, the U.S. tries to advance universal principles."[6]

Comment seems superfluous. But this is what many in enlightened circles believe. The import on policy is not obscure.

Turning to our immediate concern here, nuclear weapons policies, it is worthwhile to look carefully at how governments regard the principle that "ensuring and preserving the health and vitality of human civilization [is] their most important duty." Regrettably, governments have consistently not even considered security of their own populations as a particularly high priority.

Let's begin with the early days of the ultimate weapon, at a time when the United States had overwhelming wealth and power and remarkable security. There was, however, a potential threat: ICBMs with nuclear warheads. In his comprehensive review of nuclear policies, McGeorge Bundy describes "the timely development of ballistic missiles during the Eisenhower administration [as] one of the best achievements of those eight years. Yet it is well to begin with a recognition that both the United States and the Soviet Union might be in much less nuclear danger today if these missiles had never been developed." He then adds a remarkable comment: "I am aware of no serious contemporary proposal, in or out of either government, that ballistic missiles should somehow be banned by agreement." In short, there was apparently no thought of trying to prevent the sole serious threat to the United States—the threat of utter destruction. Rather, the institutional imperatives of state power prevailed, rather as in the case of the CEOs for whom the fate of the species is of such little concern that it does not even enter into the rankings.[7]

Could the development of these missiles have been prevented?

There might have been opportunities. One suggestive indication is a proposal by Stalin in 1952 offering to allow Germany to be unified with free elections on condition that it not join a hostile military alliance—hardly an extreme condition in the light of the history of the preceding half century.

Stalin's proposal was taken seriously by the respected political commentator James Warburg, but apart from him it was mostly ignored or ridiculed. Recent scholarship has begun to take a different view. The bitterly anti-Communist Soviet scholar Adam Ulam takes the status of Stalin's proposal to be an "unresolved mystery." Washington "wasted little effort in flatly rejecting Moscow's initiative," he writes, on grounds that "were embarrassingly unconvincing," leaving open "the basic question": "Was Stalin genuinely ready to sacrifice the newly created German Democratic Republic (GDR) on the altar of real democracy," with consequences for world peace and for American security that could have been enormous? Melvyn Leffler, reviewing recent research in Soviet archives, observes that many scholars were surprised to discover that "[Lavrentiy] Beria—the sinister, brutal head of the secret police—propos[ed] that the Kremlin offer the West a deal on the unification and neutralization of Germany," agreeing "to sacrifice the East German communist regime to reduce East-West tensions" and improve internal political and economic conditions in Russia—opportunities that were squandered in favor of securing German participation in NATO.[8]

Under the circumstances, it is not impossible that agreements might have been reached that would have protected the security of the population from the gravest threat on the horizon. But the option apparently was not considered, and possible opportunities were dismissed with ridicule, another indication of how slight a role authentic security plays in state policy. These events from the early days of the Cold War have considerable resonance today.

What happened when the Cold War ended provides instructive lessons into its actual nature. One question had to do with the fate of NATO, now that the alleged threat of Russian invasion had disappeared. Mikhail Gorbachev agreed to allow a unified Germany to join NATO—a rather significant concession—but with a quid pro quo: that NATO would not expand "one inch to the East," the phrase that was used in internal discussions, referring to East Germany. NATO at once expanded to East Germany. When Gorbachev objected, he was informed that there were only verbal commitments, nothing in writing. Clinton later expanded NATO to the borders of Russia, and as John Mearsheimer pointed out in *Foreign Affairs*, indications that Ukraine might be assimilated into the Western system, possibly even into NATO, could not fail to be threatening to any Russian leader.[9]

In late December, 2016, the Western-backed Ukrainian Parliament voted 303 to 8 to rescind the policy of "nonalignment" adopted by the ousted president, and committed Ukraine to "deepen cooperation with NATO in order to achieve the criteria required for membership in this organization."[10]

The growing crisis concerning Ukraine is no slight threat.

Returning to the 1950s, other developments revealed the low priority assigned to authentic security. When Khrushchev took office, he recognized that Russia could not compete militarily with the United States, and if Russia hoped to escape its economic backwardness and the devastating effect of the war, the arms race would have to be reversed. Accordingly, he proposed sharp mutual reductions in offensive weapons. The incoming Kennedy administration considered the offer, and rejected it, instead turning to rapid military expansion. The late Kenneth Waltz observed that the Kennedy administration "undertook the largest strategic and conventional peacetime military buildup the world has yet seen . . . even as Khrushchev was trying at once to carry through a major reduction in the conventional forces and to follow a strategy of minimum deterrence, and we did so even though the balance of strategic weapons greatly favored the United States."

Once again, the decision harmed national security while enhancing state power.[11]

How severely it harmed national security was revealed in 1962, when Khrushchev sent missiles to Cuba, partially in a foolhardy effort to right the balance, setting off what Arthur Schlesinger called "the most dangerous moment in history." There is no need to review here what happened then, though it merits careful thought.

Ten years later, Henry Kissinger called a nuclear alert in the last days of the 1973 Israel-Arab war. The purpose was to warn the Russians not to interfere with his delicate diplomatic maneuvers, designed to ensure an Israeli victory, but a limited one, so that the United States would still be in control of the region unilaterally. And the maneuvers were delicate. The United States and Russia had jointly imposed a cease-fire, but Kissinger secretly informed Israel that they could ignore it. Hence the need for the nuclear alert to frighten the Russians away. Security of the population was a matter of little concern.[12]

Ten years after that, the Reagan administration launched operations to probe Russian defenses, simulating air and naval attacks. These actions were undertaken at a very tense moment and, not surprisingly, caused great alarm in Russia, leading to a major war scare in 1983, the last time the Doomsday Clock reached three minutes before midnight. Newly released archives reveal that the danger was even more severe than historians had previously assumed. A recent U.S. intelligence study concludes that "the war scare was for real" and that U.S. intelligence may have underestimated Russian concerns and the threat of a Russian preventative nuclear strike.[13]

Recently we learned that it was even more dangerous than that. In the midst of these world-threatening developments, Russia's early-warning systems detected an incoming missile strike from the United States, sending the highest-level alert. The officer on duty, Stanislav Petrov, decided that it was a false alarm and did not transmit the warnings. That was the difference between life and death.[14]

Max Tegmark recalled that twenty years earlier, a Russian submarine commander, Vasili Arkhipov, blocked the launching of nuclear-tipped torpedos, which could have set off terminal nuclear war. We should also remember that two other commanders had authorized the launch when the three submarines were under attack by U.S. destroyers during the missile crisis. The agreement of all three was required. Yet another sign of how thin is the thread that we grasp for survival.

There are chilling estimates about failures of U.S. systems, which are surely much more reliable than the Russian ones, notably Seth Baum's recent study in the *Bulletin of the Atomic Scientists*, where he concludes, appropriately enough, that "Nuclear war is the black swan we can never see, except in that brief moment when it is killing us. We delay eliminating the risk at our own peril. Now is the time to address the threat, because now we are still alive."[15]

Reviewing his long career as a strategic weapons planner, General Lee Butler, former commander of STRATCOM, wrote he had been "among the most avid of these keepers of the faith in nuclear weapons," but it is now his "burden to declare with all of the conviction I can muster that in my judgment they served us extremely ill," outlining the reasons. He then raises a haunting question: "By what authority do succeeding generations of leaders in the nuclear-weapons states usurp the power to dictate the odds of continued life on our planet? Most urgently, why does such breathtaking audacity persist at a moment when we should stand trembling in the face of our folly and united in our commitment to abolish its most deadly manifestations?"[16]

General Butler concluded that we have so far survived the nuclear age "by some combination of skill, luck, and divine intervention, and I suspect the latter in greatest proportion."[17] These are plainly not risks that would be accepted by any sane decision maker. They are being accepted by leaders who are perfectly sane, just as the risks of environmental catastrophe are being faced with eyes open, and ignored, by the masters of the universe. All are trapped by an institutional logic that is deeply pathological and that must be cured, and quickly, if we are not to "put an end to the human race," in Russell's and Einstein's words.

10

Escalation Watch: Four Looming Flash Points Facing President Trump

Michael T. Klare

Within months of taking office, President Donald Trump is likely to face one or more major international crises, possibly entailing a risk of nuclear escalation. Not since the end of the Cold War has a new chief executive been confronted with as many potential flash points involving such a risk of explosive conflict. This proliferation of crises has been brewing for some time, but the situation appears especially ominous now given Trump's pledge to bring American military force swiftly to bear on any threats of foreign transgression. With so much at risk, it's none too soon to go on a permanent escalation watch, monitoring the major global hotspots for any sign of imminent flare-ups, hoping that early warnings (and the outcry that goes with them) might help avert catastrophe.

Looking at the world today, four areas appear to pose an especially high risk of sudden crisis and conflict: the Korean Peninsula, the South China Sea, the Baltic Sea region, and the Middle East. Each of them has been the past site of recurring clashes, and all are primed to explode early in the Trump presidency. The conflict between India and Pakistan is another looming nuclear flash point, but not one in which Donald Trump is likely to be the decisive factor, since both countries are U.S. allies, each with its own strategic value and their own grievances with the other.

Why are we seeing so many potential crises now? Is this period really different from earlier presidential transitions?

It's true that the changeover from one presidential administration to another can be a time of global uncertainty, given America's pivotal importance in world affairs and the natural inclination of rival powers to test the mettle of the country's new leader. There are, however, other factors that make this moment particularly worrisome, including the changing nature of the world order, the personalities of its key leaders, and an ominous shift in military doctrine.

Just as the United States is going through a major political transition, so is the planet at large. The sole-superpower system of the post–Cold War era is finally giving way to a multipolar, if not increasingly fragmented, world in which the United States must share the limelight with other major actors, including China, Russia, India, and Iran. Political scientists remind us that transitional periods can often prove disruptive, as "status quo" powers (in this case, the United States) resist challenges to their dominance from "revisionist" states seeking to alter the global power equation. The conflict between India and Pakistan is another looming nuclear flash point, but not one in which Donald Trump is likely to be the decisive factor, since both countries are U.S. allies, each with its own strategic value and their own grievances with the other.[1] Typically, this can entail proxy wars and other kinds of sparring over contested areas, as has recently been the case in Syria, the Baltic, and the South China Sea.

This is where the personalities of key leaders enter the equation. Though President Obama oversaw constant warfare, he was temperamentally disinclined to respond with force to every overseas crisis and provocation, fearing involvement in yet more foreign wars like Iraq and Afghanistan.[2] His critics, including Donald Trump, complained bitterly that this stance only encouraged foreign adversaries to up their game, convinced that the United States had lost its will to resist provocation.[3] In a Trump administration, as the incoming president indicated on the campaign trail, America's adversaries should expect far tougher responses. Asked in September, for instance, about an incident in the Persian Gulf in which

Iranian gunboats approached American warships in a threatening manner, he typically told reporters, "When they circle our beautiful destroyers with their little boats and make gestures that . . . they shouldn't be allowed to make, they will be shot out of the water."[4]

Although with Russia, unlike Iran, Trump has promised to improve relations, there's no escaping the fact that Vladimir Putin's urge to restore some of his country's long-lost superpower glory could lead to confrontations with NATO powers that would put the new American president in a distinctly awkward position.[5] Regarding Asia, Trump has often spoken of his intent to punish China for what he considers its predatory trade practices, a stance guaranteed to clash with President Xi Jinping's goal of restoring his country's greatness.[6] This should, in turn, generate additional possibilities for confrontation, especially in the contested South China Sea. Both Putin and Xi, moreover, are facing economic difficulties at home and view foreign adventurism as a way of distracting public attention from disappointing domestic performances.[7]

These factors alone would ensure that this is a moment of potential international crisis, but something else gives it a truly dangerous edge: a growing strategic reliance in Russia and elsewhere on the early use of nuclear weapons to overcome deficiencies in "conventional" firepower.

For the United States, with its overwhelming superiority in such firepower, nuclear weapons have lost all conceivable use except as a "deterrent" against a highly unlikely first-strike attack by an enemy power. For Russia, however, lacking the means to compete on equal terms with the West in conventional weaponry, this no longer seems reasonable. So Russian strategists, feeling threatened by the way NATO has moved ever closer to its borders, are now calling for the early use of "tactical" nuclear munitions to overpower stronger enemy forces.[8] Under Russia's latest military doctrine, major combat units are now to be trained and equipped to employ such weapons at the first sign of impending defeat, either to blackmail enemy countries into submission or annihilate them.

Following this doctrine, Russia has developed the nuclear-capable Iskander ballistic missile (a successor to the infamous "Scud" missile used by Saddam Hussein in attacks on Iran, Israel, and Saudi Arabia) and forward deployed it to Kaliningrad, a small sliver of Russian territory sandwiched between Poland and Lithuania.[9] In response, NATO strategists are discussing ways to more forcefully demonstrate the West's own capacity to use tactical nuclear arms in Europe—for example, by including more nuclear-capable bombers in future NATO exercises.[10] As a result, the "firebreak" between conventional and nuclear warfare—that theoretical barrier to escalation—seems to be narrowing, creating a situation in which every crisis involving a nuclear state may potentially prove to be a nuclear crisis.

With that in mind, consider the four most dangerous potential flash points for the new Trump administration.

Korean Peninsula

North Korea's stepped-up development of nuclear weapons and long-range ballistic missiles may present the Trump administration with its first great international challenge. In recent years, the North Koreans appear to have made substantial progress in producing such missiles and designing small nuclear warheads to fit on them.[11] In 2016, the country conducted two underground nuclear tests (its fourth and fifth since 2006), along with numerous tests of various missile systems. On September 20, it also tested a powerful rocket engine that some observers believe could be used as the first stage of an intercontinental ballistic missile (ICBM) that might someday be capable of delivering a nuclear warhead to the western United States.[12]

North Korea's erratic leader, Kim Jong-un, has repeatedly spoken of his determination to acquire nuclear weapons and the ability to use them in attacks on his adversaries, including the United States.

Following a series of missile tests in spring 2016, he insisted that his country should continue to bolster its nuclear force "both in quality and quantity," stressing "the need to get the nuclear warheads deployed for national defense always on standby so as to be fired at any moment."[13] This could mean, he added, using these weapons "in a preemptive attack." On January 1, 2017, Kim reiterated his commitment to future preemptive nuclear action, adding that his country would soon test-fire an ICBM.[14]

President Obama responded to Kim's nuclear buildup by imposing increasingly tough economic sanctions and attempting—with only limited success—to persuade China, Pyongyang's crucial ally, to use its political and economic clout to usher Kim into nuclear disarmament talks. None of this seemed to make the slightest difference, which means President Trump is faced with an increasingly well-armed North Korea that may be capable of fielding usable ICBMs within the coming years.[15]

How will Trump respond to this peril? Three options seem available to him: somehow persuade China to compel Pyongyang to abandon its nuclear quest; negotiate a disarmament deal directly with Kim, possibly even on a face-to-face basis; or engage in (presumably nonnuclear) preemptive strikes aimed at destroying the North's nuclear and missile-production capabilities.

Imposing yet more sanctions and talking with China would look suspiciously like the Obama approach, while obtaining China's cooperation would undoubtedly mean compromising on trade or the South China Sea (either of which would involve humiliating concessions for a man like Trump). Even were he to recruit Chinese president Xi as a helpmate, it's unclear that Pyongyang would be deterred. As for direct talks with Kim, Trump, unlike every previous president, has already indicated that he's willing. "I would have no problem speaking to him," he told Reuters in May 2016.[16] But what exactly would he offer the North in return for its nuclear arsenal? The withdrawal of U.S. forces from South Korea? Any such solution would leave the president looking like a patsy (inconceivable for someone whose key slogan has been "Make America Great Again").

That leaves a preemptive strike. Trump appears to have implicitly countenanced that option, too, in a recent tweet ("North Korea just stated that it is in the final stages of developing a nuclear weapon capable of reaching parts of the U.S. It won't happen!").[17] In other words, he is open to the military option, rejected in the past because of the high risk of triggering an unpredictable response from the North, including a cataclysmic invasion of South Korea (and potential attacks on U.S. troops stationed there).[18] Under the circumstances, the unpredictability not just of Kim Jong-un but also of Donald Trump leaves North Korea in the highest alert category of global crises as the new era begins.

The South China Sea

The ongoing dispute over control of the South China Sea, an area bounded by China, Malaysia, Vietnam, the Philippines, and the island of Borneo, also gives cause for alarm. Citing ancient ties to islands in those waters, China claims the entire region as part of its national maritime territory.[19] Some of the same islands are, however, also claimed by Brunei, Malaysia, Vietnam, and the Philippines. Although not claiming any territory in the region itself, the United States has a defense treaty with the Philippines, relies on free passage through the area to move its warships from bases in the Pacific to war zones in the Middle East, and of course considers itself the preeminent Pacific power and plans to keep it that way.

In the past China has clashed with local powers over possession of individual islands, but more recently has sought control over all of them. As part of that process, it has begun to convert low-lying islets and atolls under its control into military bases, equipping them with airstrips and missile defense systems.[20] This has sparked protests from Vietnam and the Philippines, which claim some of those islets, and from the United States, which insists that such Chinese moves infringe on its navy's "freedom of navigation" through international waters.[21]

President Obama responded to provocative Chinese moves in the South China Sea by ordering U.S. warships to patrol in close proximity to the islands being militarized.[22] For Trump, this has been far too minimal a response. "China's toying with us," he told David Sanger of the *New York Times* in 2016. "They are when they're building in the South China Sea. They should not be doing that but they have no respect for our country and they have no respect for our president." Asked if he was prepared to use military force in response to the Chinese buildup, he responded, "Maybe."[23]

The South China Sea may prove to be an early test of Trump's promise to fight what he views as China's predatory trade behavior and Beijing's determination to resist bullying by Washington. In December 2016, Chinese sailors seized an American underwater surveillance drone near one of the atolls claimed by China. Many observers interpreted the move as a response to Trump's decision to take a phone call of congratulations from the president of Taiwan, Tsai Ing-wen, shortly after Trump's election victory.[24] That gesture, unique in recent American presidencies, was viewed in Beijing, which considers Taiwan a renegade province, as an insult to China.[25] Any further moves by Trump to aggravate or punish China on the economic front could result in further provocations in the South China Sea, opening the possibility of a clash with U.S. air and naval forces in the region.

All this is worrisome enough, but the prospects for a clash in the South China Sea increased significantly on January 11, 2017, thanks to comments made by Rex Tillerson, the former CEO of ExxonMobil and soon-to-be secretary of state, during his confirmation hearing in Washington. Testifying before the Senate Foreign Relations Committee, he said, "We're going to have to send China a clear signal that, first, the island building stops and, second, your access to those islands also is not going to be allowed."[26] Since the

Chinese are unlikely to abandon those islands—which they consider part of their sovereign territory—just because Trump and Tillerson order them to do so, the only kind of "signal" that might carry any weight would be military action.

What form would such a confrontation take and where might it lead? At this point, no one can be sure, but once such a conflict began, room for maneuver could prove limited indeed. A U.S. effort to deny China access to the islands could involve anything from a naval blockade to air and missile attacks on the military installations built there to the sinking of Chinese warships. It's hard to imagine that Beijing would refrain from taking retaliatory steps in response, and, as one move tumbled onto the next, the two nuclear-armed countries might suddenly find themselves at the brink of full-scale war.

The Baltic Sea Area

If Hillary Clinton had been elected, Vladimir Putin would have been most likely to direct his hostility to her (and the West more generally) against the pro-Western states of the Baltic Sea region. That's because NATO forces have moved most deeply into the territory of the former Soviet Union in the Baltic states of Latvia, Estonia, and Lithuania. Although fiercely determined to protect their independence, those countries are also believed to be especially vulnerable to Russia's use of "hybrid" warfare—involving covert operations, disinformation campaigns, cyberattacks, and the like—witnessed in Crimea and Ukraine.[27] With Donald Trump promising to improve relations with Moscow, it's less likely that Putin will launch such attacks, though the Russians continue to strengthen their military assets (including their nuclear warfighting capabilities) in the region, so the risk of a future clash cannot be ruled out.[28]

The danger there arises from geography, history, and policy. The three Baltic republics were incorporated into the Soviet Union after World War II and only regained their independence after the breakup of the USSR in 1991; today, they are members of both the European Union and NATO. Two of them, Estonia and Latvia, share borders with Russia proper, while Lithuania and nearby Poland surround the Russian enclave of Kaliningrad. Through their NATO membership, they provide a theoretical bridgehead for a hypothetical Western invasion of Russia. By the same token, the meager forces of the three republics could easily be overwhelmed by superior Russian ones, leaving the rest of NATO to decide whether and in what fashion to confront a Russian assault on member nations.

Following Russia's intervention in eastern Ukraine, which demonstrated Moscow's willingness and ability to engage in hybrid warfare against a neighboring European state, the NATO powers decided to bolster the alliance's forward presence in the Baltic region. At a summit meeting in Warsaw in June 2016, the alliance agreed to deploy four reinforced multinational battalions in Poland and the three Baltic republics.[29] Russia views this with alarm as a dangerous violation of promises made to Moscow in the wake of the Cold War that no NATO forces would be permanently garrisoned on the territory of the former Soviet Union.[30] NATO has tried to deflect Russian complaints by insisting that, since the four battalions will be rotated in and out of the region, they are somehow not "permanent." Nevertheless, from Moscow's perspective, the NATO move represents a serious threat to Russian security and so justifies a comparable buildup of Russian forces in adjacent areas.[31]

Adding to the obvious dangers of such a mutual buildup, NATO and Russian forces have been conducting elaborate military "exercises," often in close proximity to each other. In the summer of 2016, for example, NATO oversaw Anaconda 2016 in Poland and Lithuania, the largest such maneuvers in the region since the end of the Cold War. As part of the exercise, NATO forces crossed from

Poland to Lithuania, making clear their ability to encircle Kaliningrad, which was bound to cause deep unease in Moscow.[32] Not
that the Russians have been passive. During related NATO naval
exercises in the Baltic Sea, Russian planes flew within a few feet
of an American warship, the USS *Donald Cook*, nearly provoking a
shooting incident that could have triggered a far more dangerous
confrontation.[33]

Will Putin ease up on the pressure he's been exerting on the Baltic states now that Trump is in power? Will Trump agree to cancel
or downsize the U.S. and NATO deployments there in return for
Russian acquiescence on other issues? Such questions will be on the
minds of many in Eastern Europe in the coming months. It's reasonable to predict a period of relative calm as Putin tests Trump's
willingness to forge a new relationship with Moscow, but the underlying stresses will remain as long as the Baltic states stay in NATO
and Russia views that as a threat to its security.

The Middle East

The Middle East has long been a major flash point. President
Obama, for instance, came to office hoping to end U.S. involvement
in wars in Iraq and Afghanistan, yet U.S. troops are still fighting
in both countries today. The question is: How might this picture
change in the months ahead?

Given the convoluted history of the region and its demonstrated
capacity for surprise, any predictions should be offered with cau-
tion. Trump has promised to intensify the war against ISIS, which
will undoubtedly require the deployment of additional American
air, sea, and ground forces in the region. As he put it during the
election campaign, speaking of the Islamic State, "I would bomb
the shit out of them."[34] So expect accelerated air strikes on ISIS-held
locations, leading to more civilian casualties, desperate migrants,
and heightened clashes between Shiites and Sunnis.[35] As ISIS loses
control of physical territory and returns to guerrilla-style warfare,

it will surely respond by increasing terrorist attacks on "soft" civilian targets in neighboring Iraq, Jordan, and Turkey, as well as in more distant locations.[36] No one knows how all this will play out, but don't be surprised if terrorist violence only increases and Washington once again finds itself drawn more deeply into an endless quagmire in the greater Middle East and northern Africa.

The overriding question, of course, is how Donald Trump will behave toward Iran. He has repeatedly affirmed his opposition to the nuclear deal signed by the United States, the European Union, Russia, and China and insisted that he would either scrap it or renegotiate it, but it's hard to imagine how that might come to pass.[37] All of the other signatories are satisfied with the deal and seek to do business with Iran, so any new negotiations would have to proceed without those parties. As many U.S. strategists also see merit in the agreement, since it deprives Iran of a nuclear option for at least a decade or more, a decisive shift on the nuclear deal appears unlikely.[38]

On the other hand, Trump could be pressured by his close associates—especially his top political strategist, Stephen K. Bannon, a notoriously outspoken Islamophobe—to counter the Iranians on other fronts.[39] This could take a variety of forms, including stepped-up sanctions, increased aid to Saudi Arabia in its war against the Iranian-backed Houthis in Yemen, or attacks on Iranian proxies in the Middle East. Any of these would no doubt prompt countermoves by Tehran, and from there a cycle of escalation could lead in numerous directions, all dangerous, including military action by the United States, Israel, or Saudi Arabia.

Going on Watch

When Donald Trump took office on January 20, 2017, the clock began ticking in each of these flash-point regions. No one knows which will be the first to erupt, or what will happen when it does, but don't count on escape from all of the major international crises we can expect in the not-too-distant future.

Given the stakes involved, it's essential to keep a close watch on all of them for signs of anything that might trigger a major conflagration and for indications of a prematurely violent Trumpian response (the moment to raise a hue and cry). Keeping the spotlight shining on these four potential flash points may not be much, but it's the least we can do to avert Armageddon.

11

Nuclear Politics

William D. Hartung

The term military-industrial complex dates back to President Dwight D. Eisenhower's 1961 farewell address to the nation. The concepts set out in that speech remain relevant, more than fifty years later. But although the military-industrial complex is a powerful force, it is not an immovable obstacle. It is a product of society and it can be dismantled by society, given adequate focus, determination, and commitment.

Why did Eisenhower, a general, a war hero, and the first Republican president of the Cold War era, choose to focus his last remarks as president on the issue of the military-industrial complex? The first reason Eisenhower gave the speech was that he thought the military-industrial complex was a relatively new phenomenon of unprecedented power that we ignored at our peril: "The conjunction of an immense military establishment and a large arms industry is new in the American experience. The total influence—economic, political, even spiritual—is felt in every city, every statehouse, every office of the federal government."[1]

He went on to utter the most famous phrase from the speech, the need to "guard against the acquisition of unwarranted influence, whether sought or unsought, by the military-industrial complex."[2] It was necessary to do something about this new development. It could not be allowed to grow unchecked to the point that it became the dominant force in our society. Ultimately, Eisenhower felt the military-industrial complex was a threat to democracy, saying, "We must never let the weight of this combination endanger our liberties or democratic processes. We should take nothing for granted. Only an alert and knowledgeable citizenry can compel the proper meshing of the huge industrial machinery of defense with our peaceful methods and goals, so that security and liberty may prosper together."[3]

Without the development of nuclear weapons, the military-industrial complex would not exist in the form that it exists today. We should note that the Manhattan Project of the 1940s was one of the largest government-funded research and manufacturing projects in history, and today's nuclear warhead complex is built largely around facilities and locations that date back to that time.[4] The Manhattan Project was the first building block of the "permanent arms establishment" that concerned Eisenhower.

But it wasn't just that the nuclear weapons complex was one of the first important elements of the military-industrial complex. The nuclear arms race was a central part of the rationale for sustaining a permanent arms establishment in the first place. Eisenhower noted in his speech that we developed a "permanent arms industry of vast proportions" because "we can no longer risk emergency improvisation of national defense."[5] We could no longer "improvise" because in an era of potential nuclear warfare our society could be destroyed in a matter of hours; there would be no time to mobilize for war.

The logic of the time was that the entire military establishment, most important our nuclear arsenal, had to be on a hair trigger to prevent the other side from acting first. While there was an overall dangerous illogic in the Cold War nuclear weapons buildup, I am addressing only the specific role of nuclear weapons in the genesis of the military-industrial complex as a whole.

There were some very specific ways in which nuclear weapons and nuclear delivery vehicles drove Eisenhower to give his military-industrial complex speech. One of Eisenhower's biggest fights with the arms establishment was over whether to build a new nuclear bomber. The air force and the industry wanted one. Eisenhower thought it was a waste of money, and redundant, given all the other nuclear delivery vehicles the United States was building at that time.[6] Eisenhower ultimately won the battle over the bomber, but he and his administration lost the larger war to rein in the nation's nuclear buildup.

At the same time as the fight over the new bomber, there were rumblings in the intelligence community, the military establishment, the media, and Congress about a "missile gap" with the Soviet Union—the notion that Moscow was poised to jump ahead of the United States in developing and building long-range ballistic missiles. There was no definitive intelligence to prove this claim, but a wave of worst-case scenarios emanating from intelligence analysts in the air force and other agencies brought the notion of a missile gap into the public discourse. These fears were then exaggerated and widely disseminated, aided by hawkish journalists such as Joseph Alsop and prominent Democratic senators such as John F. Kennedy of Massachusetts, Stuart Symington of Missouri, and Lyndon Johnson of Texas. Kennedy gave a widely circulated speech about the missile gap on the Senate floor, and made it a central theme of his 1960 campaign for the presidency. Symington was a friend and former colleague of an executive at Convair, and he lobbied on behalf of a plan to build more of the company's Atlas ballistic missiles.[7]

Eisenhower viewed the missile gap as a fiction, but he saw the issue as "a useful piece of political demagoguery" for his opponents. Eisenhower said that "munitions makers are making tremendous efforts toward getting more contracts, and in fact seem to be exerting undue influence over the Senators"—a situation that continues to this day.[8]

Kennedy had another reason for promoting the missile gap thesis: pork-barrel politics. In his book on Kennedy, Christopher Preble noted that "Kennedy intended his message tying foreign policy and national security to domestic economic issues to resonate particularly well with one group of voters, defense workers."[9] There was only one problem—there was no missile gap. In fact, once Kennedy took office, it became apparent that any missile gap that might exist was in favor of the United States.[10]

Historians differ on whether Kennedy knew that the missile gap was a fiction during his campaign for president, or if he only learned of it once he took office.[11] Regardless of when Kennedy knew, it was clear that a combination of fear, hyped intelligence, and special-interest pleading had set the stage for a new military buildup. This pattern repeated itself throughout the Cold War and on into the 2000s.

The end of the Cold War and the disintegration of the Soviet Union offered a possibility to dramatically scale back, if not eliminate, the military-industrial complex. Colin Powell, in 1991, as head of the Joint Chiefs of Staff, noted, "I'm running out of enemies."[12] There were no threats on the horizon that could justify spending the kind of money that was spent when the Soviet Union was U.S. adversary number one. But a solution was soon found. The Pentagon focused on smaller potential adversaries like Iraq and North Korea, and argued that in the event that the United States had to fight two of these powers simultaneously, it would need almost as large a military as it would take to deal with the Soviet Union. Pentagon spending still came down substantially—about one-third during the first half of the 1990s—but it didn't come down nearly as far as it should have given the state of the world. The "regional threats" argument kept the Pentagon budget much higher than it needed to be to defend the country.[13]

As post–Cold War Pentagon spending came down, the seeds of the next buildup were being sown. During the administration of George W. Bush, an internal Pentagon strategy document suggested that rather than seek a peace dividend at the end of the Cold War, the United States should double down on military spending to ensure that it had unrivaled dominance, not just over potential adversaries but over potential allies as well. When this information was leaked, it caused great consternation among U.S. allies in Europe, and the Pentagon essentially renounced the findings of its own internal document. But the architects of that document, many of whom went on to join the Bush administration, never gave up their vision of unrivaled U.S. military dominance.

During the latter half of the 1990s, advocates of a more aggressive U.S. foreign policy and a huge boost in Pentagon spending organized themselves into groups like the Project for the New American Century (PNAC), which called for things like a return to a "Reaganite policy of military strength" and an active military campaign to overthrow Saddam Hussein's regime in Iraq. Members of the project included future officials of George W. Bush's administration Dick Cheney, Donald Rumsfeld, Paul Wolfowitz, and Richard Perle. But PNAC was composed of more than just pro-Pentagon ideologues. Its original director was Bruce Jackson, a vice president at the Lockheed Martin Corporation.[14]

Even members of PNAC could not have imagined how much of their agenda would be carried out in the following decade. In one of their documents they suggested that the only thing that would motivate the public to support their agenda in full would be a "catastrophic event" like a "new Pearl Harbor."[15] September 11 was that event. The advocates of overthrowing Saddam Hussein and ratcheting up Pentagon spending seized on the atmosphere of fear that followed the September 11 attacks to promote the invasion of Iraq— sold, as we now know, on false claims that Saddam Hussein had weapons of mass destruction. This was not a case of conspiracy—it was a case of a group with a preexisting agenda seizing a historical moment that was favorable to the promotion of their views, a particularly costly case of political opportunism. In parallel with the Iraq and Afghan war buildups, U.S. military spending increased to its highest levels since World War II. From 1998 to 2010, the Pentagon budget increased every year, the longest uninterrupted string of budgetary growth in its history.[16]

When we think of special-interest lobbies today, we often focus on the flood of private money that is corrupting our political process, from the Koch brothers and their radical right-wing agenda to the financial and pharmaceutical industries that are at the top of the list of corporate campaign donors. The arms industry is also a major campaign donor, but its contributions are relatively small compared to those of Wall Street or individuals like the Koch brothers.[17] It has so many other avenues of influence that it need not rely as heavily on political giving as some other sectors. Let's look at what some of those tools are, starting with campaign spending and then moving on to even more powerful, insidious forms of leverage exerted by the arms industry.

In campaign financing, the defense sector has contributed nearly $50 million to candidates for Congress in the past three election cycles, since 2009. The bulk of these funds go to members of the armed services and defense appropriations subcommittees—members who can make a difference in funding decisions about particular weapons programs or military facilities. The second most favored group—which overlaps substantially the first—is members who have significant weapons factories or military bases in their state or congressional district. Together these members make up a formidable coalition in favor of high Pentagon budgets and specific weapons programs.

The biggest recipient of campaign cash from the arms lobby in recent years has been former House Armed Services Committee chair Howard P. "Buck" McKeon (R-CA), who received three-quarters of a million dollars from arms companies in the last three election cycles, and whose top donors routinely included major defense contractors like Lockheed Martin and Northrop Grumman.[18] When McKeon announced his retirement in 2014, the industry immediately shifted gears and started pouring contributions into the coffers of his successor as Armed Services Committee chair, Rep. Mac Thornberry (R-TX).[19] The arms industry's campaign spending strategy is as much about targeting the most powerful members as it is about the absolute amounts of money contributed.

The largest area of expenditures designed to exert influence over Congress and the executive branch is direct lobbying funding. The defense industry as a whole spent $680 million on lobbying over the past five years, and has on average anywhere from eight hundred to over one thousand lobbyists—nearly two lobbyists for every member of Congress.[20] The vast majority of these lobbyists formerly worked at the Pentagon, the Department of Energy, or on key congressional committees. This brings us to the issue of the revolving door—a long-standing practice of companies and other interest groups that want an inside track on influencing government. The late senator William Proxmire of Wisconsin gave one of the best explanations of the insidiousness of the revolving door:

> The easy movement of high ranking military officers into jobs with major defense contractors and the reverse movements of top executives in major defense contractors into high Pentagon jobs is solid evidence of the military-industrial complex in action. It is a real threat to the public interest because it increases the chances of abuse. . . . How hard a bargain will officers involved in procurement planning or specifications drive when they are one or two years from retirement and have the example to look at of over 2,000 fellow officers doing well on the outside after retirement?[21]

Proxmire was speaking in 1969, so this is hardly a new phenomenon. A few years back, Bryan Bender of the *Boston Globe* did an analysis of what happened to three- and four-star generals and admirals once they left the government, and he found that thirty-four of thirty-nine of them went to work for Pentagon contractors or set up defense consulting firms.[22] At the high end of the scale, it's not a question of who is going through the revolving door, it's more a question of who is not.

Another way the nuclear weapons industry in particular and the military-industrial complex in general try to control the public debate is by funding hawkish, right-wing think tanks. The advantage to contractors of operating in this fashion is that the think tanks can serve as front groups that pose as objective policy analysts when in fact they are carrying water for the industry. It's sort of like political money laundering—but it's political idea laundering. There are many examples of think tanks that are funded by the weapons industry.

My favorite industry-funded right-wing think tank is Frank Gaffney's Center for Security Policy, which has been the biggest booster of the Star Wars program since shortly after Ronald Reagan announced it in the mid-1980s. Mr. Gaffney served with Richard Perle, known informally as the "Prince of Darkness" because of his gloomy view of the Soviet Union. Gaffney left the Reagan administration because they weren't anti-Soviet enough for him once they started talking about things like reducing nuclear weapons in Europe. It didn't take him long to set up his center with funding from Boeing, Lockheed, and other major defense contractors.[23]

Another key industry-backed think tank in the nuclear policy field is the National Institute for Public Policy. When the George W. Bush administration was coming into power, this institute released a report on nuclear weapons policy that was adopted in large part by the Bush administration in its first nuclear posture review. It included things like increasing the number of countries targeted by U.S. nuclear weapons and building new, more "usable," bunker-busting weapons. At that time NIPP had an executive from Boeing on its board, and its director was Keith Payne, infamous in the annals of nuclear policy for a 1980 article he co-authored for *Foreign Policy* magazine entitled "Victory Is Possible," about how the United States could win a nuclear war while "only" losing 30 to 40 million people.[24] This is the kind of person the nuclear weapons industry funded to promulgate its views.

Last but not least is the Lexington Institute, the think tank that never met a weapons system it didn't like. Their key front man, Loren Thompson, is frequently quoted in news stories on defense issues. It is rarely pointed out that he is funded by Lockheed Martin, Northrop Grumman, and other weapons contractors.[25]

When traditional lobbying methods don't get the job done, the industry's argument of last resort is jobs—in particular, jobs in the states and districts of key members of Congress. The industry routinely exaggerates the number of jobs its activities creates—virtually any other activity will create significantly more jobs than Pentagon spending. A study by economists at the University of Massachusetts found that a tax cut would create 25 percent more jobs than Pentagon spending; infrastructure investment would create one and one-half times as many jobs; and education spending would create more than twice as many jobs.[26] But even if the industry exaggerates the numbers, the jobs argument is still potent in states and communities that depend on Pentagon spending for a significant portion of their economic activity.

Nuclear weapons facilities are spread throughout the country. There are nuclear weapons labs in California and New Mexico; a nuclear weapons test site and research site in Nevada; a nuclear warhead assembly and disassembly plant in Texas; a factory in Kansas City, Missouri, that builds the nonnuclear parts of nuclear weapons; a plant in South Carolina that reprocesses nuclear-weapons-grade materials to create fuel for nuclear reactors; and a plant in Oak Ridge, Tennessee, that enriches uranium for nuclear weapons. There are factories or bases for ICBMs, nuclear bombers, and ballistic missile submarines in Connecticut, Georgia, Washington State, Southern California, Ohio, Massachusetts, Louisiana, North Dakota, Montana, and Wyoming.[27] That's a lot of members of Congress to stand up in favor of spending on nuclear weapons.

But it's important to know that the majority of states and districts do not contain nuclear weapons activities. The challenge is to organize members from these states, a task that may be made easier by the fact that the Pentagon currently plans to spend an astounding $1 trillion on researching, building, and operating nuclear weapons over the next three decades.[28] That money will have to come from somewhere—members whose districts are starved for basic services and deficit hawks who want to shrink the government could build a "strange bedfellows" coalition to stop this spending.

Finally, there are what could be called party favors—things the companies do to advance the personal interests of members. For example, the late representative Jack Murtha, a Democrat from Pennsylvania, was considered the king of pork-barrel politics in the House of Representatives. He could steer Pentagon spending to your district if you got on his good side, and he could try to cut it off if you opposed him on things he cared about. And what he cared about most was getting Pentagon money to companies in his district.[29] So he got hundreds of thousands in campaign contributions from Pentagon contractors, and companies like Lockheed Martin put factories in his district. But one of the most interesting strategies had nothing to do with building weapons—it had to do with making music.

Johnstown, Pennsylvania, in Murtha's congressional district, had one of the best symphony orchestras in the country. There was a reason for that. It was the favorite charity of Jack Murtha's wife, and it got major contributions every year from big Pentagon contractors like Lockheed Martin and Northrop Grumman as a way to curry favor with Murtha.[30] Perfectly legal, but clearly a form of influence peddling.

Another case was the Trent Lott Leadership Institute at the University of Mississippi. When Mississippi's Lott was Senate majority leader, the university set up an institute in his honor. One of the biggest contributors to the institute was Lockheed Martin, to the tune of $1 million.[31]

One more example will underscore the point. Until 2014, Howard P. "Buck" McKeon (R-CA) was the head of the House Armed Services Committee. His district was full of factories and research facilities that worked on everything from drones to the stealth coating on the F-35 fighter plane. His top campaign donors were Boeing, Lockheed Martin, and the other major Pentagon contractors. He was practically a one-man military-industrial complex. As with Jack Murtha and Trent Lott, the traditional methods of influence weren't enough for these companies. They found another way to get in Buck McKeon's good graces. His wife Patricia decided to run for the California state legislature, and Lockheed Martin contributed generously to her campaign.[32] The company swore that this had nothing to do with influencing Buck McKeon, that they had just taken a sudden interest in state and local issues. As Patricia McKeon's main issue was an effort to repeal a ten-cent tax on plastic bags, Lockheed Martin's explanation that it somehow cared about this issue didn't pass the laugh test.[33] Still, everything they did to help Patricia McKeon was legal—just another form of influence peddling.

There is a common assumption that the military-industrial complex is all-powerful—that it will always get what it wants and there's nothing we can do about it—therefore, we shouldn't even bother trying to fight it. This is not true. There have been a number of cases in recent years where activists have been able to stop the complex from getting what it wants.

One example was the F-22 fighter plane—the most expensive fighter plane ever built by the Pentagon. When the Obama administration wanted to end the program, Lockheed Martin, the prime contractor on the plane, jumped into action. They got forty-four senators and two hundred members of the House of Representatives to send letters to President Obama asking him to keep funding the plane. They also got the governors of twelve states to weigh in, including the Democratic governors of New York and Ohio. They made the usual claims that the F-22 was a major jobs program—95,000 jobs nationwide, they claimed. They also conducted a major ad campaign touting the plane.[34]

Normally all of this activity would have been enough to keep the F-22 going years beyond when the Pentagon wanted to end the program. But a coalition of peace and arms control groups organized against the plane, and the president and the secretary of defense spoke out against it. John McCain agreed with Obama that the F-22 should be stopped—one of the few things they agreed on. And President Obama threatened to veto any defense bill that included funding for the F-22. As a result, Lockheed Martin lost the vote to save the plane by a healthy margin—58 to 40 in the Senate. A lot of senators didn't buy the jobs argument, didn't think the plane was needed, or, in the case of some Republican deficit hawks—including Tea Party favorites like Senator Jim DeMint of South Carolina—just thought it was too expensive. So Lockheed Martin, the biggest weapons contractor in the world, lost this battle.[35]

More recently, the arms industry has lost the battle over how much to spend on the Pentagon. The Pentagon's base budget has come down by over 10 percent in the past few years, despite a campaign by the Aerospace Industries Association claiming that the country would lose a million jobs if the cuts went through.[36] But the cuts did go through, by and large, and national employment actually increased. So the arms lobby's credibility took a hit on Capitol Hill.

It's important to look at the context of recent cuts in Pentagon spending; the Department of Defense base budget is still about one-half trillion dollars a year, so the Pentagon is hardly starved for funds. As of early 2016, the department was on track to get over $500 billion less over a decade's time than was projected in Secretary of Defense Robert Gates's Fiscal Year 2012 budget. But that will still leave the Pentagon with well over $5 trillion for the decade. That's a lot of money even by Pentagon standards. But even at those enormous levels of spending, the Pentagon will not be able to afford its wish list, so it will have to give something up.[37]

As a result, in recent years the Pentagon has offset some of the cuts in its base budget by adding equipment and activities to the war budget that have nothing to do with fighting wars. The war budget—known in Pentagon-ese as the Overseas Contingency Operations (OCO) account—is supposed to pay for items directly related to the wars in Iraq and Afghanistan. But in the past few years the Pentagon has added $20 billion to $30 billion a year to the OCO account that is completely unrelated to supporting or carrying out current conflicts. The war budget has in essence operated as a "slush fund" to soften the blow of cuts in the Pentagon's base budget.[38] Even allowing for the OCO slush fund, Pentagon spending is on course to be many hundreds of billions of dollars less over the next decade than the Pentagon was expecting just a few years ago. As a result, the Pentagon can no longer afford all of the weapons and activities in its long-term plan.

Why has the Pentagon's base budget gone down? Because of political gridlock in Washington. When Republicans threatened to shut down the government in the summer of 2011, a compromise was reached, in the form of the Budget Control Act. The Budget Control Act said that Pentagon and domestic spending other than entitlements like Medicare and Social Security would be capped for a ten-year period, unless the Congress and the president could agree on a major deficit reduction plan. The theory was that the caps would be so unattractive to both parties that they would come together and agree on a mix of revenue increases and program cuts that would reduce the deficit without having to cap Pentagon and domestic spending. But over three years later, there has been no such agreement. Republicans refuse to raise taxes and Democrats by and large oppose cuts in Medicare and Social Security. So the reductions in Pentagon spending were carried out, and there was little that the arms lobby could do about it. If the caps continue, it will be impossible for the Pentagon to afford things like its $1 trillion nuclear weapons spending plan, which will have to be substantially reduced.

This is not to say that the military-industrial complex isn't powerful, just that it's not all-powerful. An upsurge of citizen pressure combined with a "strange bedfellows" coalition of liberal Democrats and deficit hawk conservatives can force further cuts in Pentagon spending. The first thing to go has to be the Pentagon's $1 trillion plan to build a new generation of nuclear-armed missiles, submarines, and bombers over the next three decades. Despite issues relating to the special-interest politics of Pentagon spending decisions in Washington and around the country, as this book suggests, there is much more at stake than money. We are talking about the future of humanity, and people will ultimately need to be moved to action by that reality if we are going to reverse the nuclear buildup.

12

Ignition Points for Global Catastrophe: A Legacy of U.S. Foreign Policy

Richard Broinowski

In 1920, H.L. Mencken wrote prophetically that "as democracy is perfected, the office of the President represents, more and more closely, the inner soul of the people. On some grand and glorious day, the plain folks of the land will reach their heart's desire at last, and the White House will be occupied by a downright fool and a complete narcissistic moron."[1]

To the dismay of more than half the world, Donald Trump was elected forty-fifth president of the United States on November 8, 2016. His campaign was a triumph of emotional populism over rationality. Without apology he displayed racism and misogyny, contempt for social welfare and the science of climate change. He proudly proclaimed himself to be an isolationist and trade protectionist, a pro-gun lobbyist who was relaxed about the use of tactical nuclear weapons.

Political commentators immediately began scrambling to try to make sense of the sweeping, often contradictory, foreign policy agenda Trump had announced piecemeal during his debates with Hillary Clinton and in thirty-second grabs throughout the presidential campaign. Among his more coherent pronouncements were that he would impose massive tariffs on Chinese imports into the United States. He would abolish long-standing security agreements the United States had with Japan and the Republic of Korea, thus withdrawing the protection of the American nuclear umbrella. Both countries, he said, should become self-reliant and develop their own nuclear arsenals if they felt so inclined. In the Middle East he would tear up the Joint Comprehensive Plan of Action (JCPOA) between the permanent five UN Security Council members and Germany on one hand and Iran on the other. He would destroy ISIS in Syria and Iraq through a massive bombing campaign. In Europe he would negotiate some form of rapprochement with Russia and review U.S. defense commitments to the twenty-eight member states of NATO on the grounds that the treaty was obsolete, costing the United States a fortune. At home, he would build a wall between Mexico and the United States, abrogate the North America Free Trade Agreement (NAFTA), and substantially increase the size of U.S. armed forces.

Extravagant claims more compatible with a media showman than a considered statesman made in the heat of electoral battle are one thing; enforcing them after electoral victory is quite another. An optimistic speculation is that Trump's rhetoric was for show, and that, guided by wise and sober counsel, he will change his tune as an incumbent. At this stage it is too early to know which of his plans he will implement, but the international political and military situation is fragile enough without Trump's threatened destabilizing interventions. For he has inherited at least five situations, four of which are the result of direct or indirect U.S. policies, that could lead to nuclear war. The theaters are in Northern Europe, the Middle East, the Indian subcontinent, the South China Sea, and North Asia. There may be others, but let us stick to what we know.

Russia

The situation in Northern Europe involves Russia and NATO. At its formation in 1949, NATO consisted of twelve Western European countries. Greece, Turkey, West Germany, and Spain joined between 1952 and 1982, but the organization's wholesale expansion into Eastern Europe was yet to come. In December 1988, Mikhail

Gorbachev proposed to incoming U.S. president George H.W. Bush sweeping reforms—characterized by the *New York Times* as the greatest act of statesmanship since Wilson's Fourteen Points in 1918, or Roosevelt's and Churchill's Atlantic Charter of 1941.[2] The reforms included the dissolution of NATO as well as the Warsaw Pact, both Cold War relics. If NATO continued to exist, Gorbachev insisted that it should not be permitted to expand eastward. Russia wanted a cordon sanitaire of neutral states between NATO forces and Russia's western borders. At "2 + 4 Talks" in 1990 between representatives of East and West Germany (the 2), France, the United Kingdom, the United States, and the Soviet Union (the 4), it was agreed that foreign troops and nuclear weapons would not be stationed in the former East Germany. In his memoir, Jack Matlock, U.S. ambassador to the Soviet Union between 1987 and 1991, specifically recalls the undertaking.[3] And in his own memoir published in 1996, Mikhail Gorbachev goes further, claiming that France, Britain, and the United States all gave assurances that NATO would not extend its zone of operations to the east.[4] The Clinton administration (1993–2001) and the George W. Bush administration (2002–2009) allegedly confirmed these assurances, but despite volumes of academic research and analysis, neither assertion has ever been proven beyond doubt. Meanwhile, against strategic logic, and in a manner highly provocative to the new Federation of Russian States, NATO's membership ineluctably expanded. Poland, Hungary, and the Czech Republic joined in 1999, Bulgaria, Estonia, Latvia, Lithuania, Romania, Slovakia, and Slovenia in 2004, and Albania and Croatia in 2009. By 2012, NATO had twenty-eight members, with Ukraine petitioning to join. Ukraine initially applied to do so in 2008 but, following the election of the non-aligned candidate Viktor Yanukovych, withdrew the bid. Indeed, polls conducted between 2005 and 2013 showed that 50 percent of Ukrainians did not want Ukraine associated with NATO.[5] In 2014, however, Yanukovych fled the country. Exiled in Russia, he is currently wanted by Ukraine on charges of high treason. His successor,

Petro Poroshenko, initially had no plans to join NATO, but Russian occupation of Crimea and territorial intervention in Ukraine in the same year changed the political climate and Ukrainians felt threatened. Following a referendum and national elections, President Poroshenko's government renewed Ukraine's earlier bid to join. At the time of this writing, Ukraine's membership has not been formalized, but the United States under President Obama aggressively increased American military assistance to Kiev. Bills Obama signed in December 2015 provided $658 million for training, equipment, weapons "of a defensive nature," logistical support, military supplies and services, and intelligence support. The U.S. administration also lifted a forty-year ban on the export of crude petroleum to Ukraine in an attempt to reduce Ukraine's reliance on Russian oil.

In the face of NATO encroachment and U.S. military assistance to Ukraine, the Russians have aggressively pushed back, not just in the South, but across Europe in general. Russian troops have entered eastern Ukraine. Putin has modernized Russian missiles and submarines, reintroduced regular bomber patrols in international airspace, especially in the Baltic, and expanded Russian territorial claims in the Arctic. The United States is placing missile defense sites in Poland and the Czech Republic. The threat exists of miscalculation or accident leading to the launch of missiles on hair-trigger alert. The Cold War has returned to haunt Europe in a new, potentially hot form. Across the whole European theater, Russian and NATO forces are most likely to clash over the Baltic States or Ukraine. General Sir Richard Shirreff, former second-in-command of NATO forces, poses two likely scenarios in his book *War with Russia: An Urgent Warning from Senior Military Command.*[6] One scenario is Latvia's Russian-speaking minority in Riga being infiltrated by Russian special forces, who engineer chaos, providing the excuse for Russian airborne troops arriving from the Russian oblast of Pskov, twenty kilometers east of the Estonian border. Latvia, Estonia, and Lithuania are all NATO members, and NATO forces would have to react, leading to a direct confrontation between them and Russian forces. Another possibility is the Russian army sweeping westward toward Kiev from the pro-Russian Ukrainian provinces of Donetsk or Luhansk. Ukraine is not yet a member of NATO, but the organization may well retaliate. Either or both scenarios could rapidly degenerate into a nuclear exchange.

What should Trump do? He could immediately communicate with Vladimir Putin and negotiate a deal to defuse tensions. (He says he's good at deals.) He could offer to withdraw NATO interceptor missiles based in Poland and a radar system installed in the Czech Republic. He could offer Putin assurances that he would not encourage NATO to accept Ukraine as a member. What may he be *inclined* to do? We don't yet know and current sustained discussions by academics and political analysts across the Western world have produced no answers. But there are some elusive grounds for optimism that he may not be as confrontational toward Russia as Hillary Clinton would have been. It is every sensible person's hope that the drift toward military confrontation with the Russians in Europe will be avoided.

The Middle East

The Middle East is an unstable mess, a perfect storm, a trigger for further nuclear confrontation. The genie of sectarian violence escaped the bottle in 2003, when the United States and its so-called "Coalition of the Willing" (mainly Britain, Poland, and Australia) illegally invaded Iraq against all kinds of informed and sober intelligence that Saddam Hussein was not harboring weapons of mass destruction. Saddam Hussein was killed, his secular Ba'ath government dismissed, his army disbanded, his infrastructure destroyed. Shiite rose against Sunni, and pro-Sunni extremists, mainly ex-soldiers, created ISIS. No weapons of mass destruction were found.

In 2011, a fruit seller immolated himself in Tunisia because the Tunisian government kept hounding him for taxes. This incendiary action led to the so-called Arab Spring, in which uprisings occurred against corrupt and repressive governments across the region. In the following year, the Arab Spring reached Syria, where a disparate collection of rebels began armed resistance against the government of Bashar al-Assad. The struggle quickly degenerated into a series of overlapping proxy wars. Assad's Ba'ath regime is supported by Iran, Russia—the only major power with military forces openly stationed in Syria—Hezbollah, and Palestine; the opposing Syrian National Coalition has support from Saudi Arabia, Qatar, and Turkey. The United States, France, the UK, and Australia selectively support rebel groups fighting Assad while at the same time attempting to contain depredations of the Islamic State of Iraq and the Levant (ISIL or ISIS). In April 2017, in response to a chemical weapons attack by Assad that left over 100 Syrians dead, President Trump fired 59 missiles at the al-Shayrat military air base in Syria, destroying the military base that launched the gas attack.

Clashes have already occurred between Turkey (a NATO member) and Russia, and it is quite likely that a direct confrontation could occur between Russian and U.S. air forces, which could in turn lead to a wider clash between these two powers. In view of President Trump's cavalier attitude toward the use of nuclear weapons, it is entirely possible that a nuclear exchange could follow.

Another potential Middle Eastern flash point exists in Iran. The Joint Comprehensive Plan of Action (JCPOA), or "Iran deal," was painstakingly negotiated over twenty months from 2013 to 2015 between the five permanent members of the Security Council and Germany on the one hand and Iran on the other. The deal has actually been quite effective in limiting Iran's nuclear weapons aspirations. Measures to be taken include eliminating the country's stockpile of medium-enriched uranium 235, cutting its stockpile of low-enriched uranium 235 by 98 percent, reducing its inventory of gas centrifuges by two-thirds, enriching uranium by only 3.67 percent for the next fifteen years, building no heavy water reactors for the next fifteen years, and restricting its enrichment facilities to one facility using only first-generation centrifuges. All such measures are to be monitored on a regular basis by the International Atomic Energy Agency, a process that has been in place for two years now. It has been calculated that any covert intention by Iran to develop nuclear weapons (and such an intention is far from proven) has been delayed by at least ten more years, possibly longer. And yet Israel fiercely opposes the deal, and so does Donald Trump. During his many campaign speeches he has characterized the deal as the "stupidest of all time, absolutely giving Iran a bomb-making capacity, changing it from a failed state to a big power."[7] (In an irrelevant and bizarre aside, he also wondered when Iran "will do something to halt the developing nuclear weapons capacity of North Korea."[8]) Will Trump walk away from the JCPOA and reimpose crippling economic sanctions? If he does, will the other members of the P5 or Germany follow suit? If they do (which is very doubtful), will Iran simply build back its nuclear capacity and (like North Korea)proceed with a nuclear weapons program? Would Israel stand by or carry out its often-repeated threat to bomb Iran? If Iran did proceed with such a program, could Saudi Arabia, Egypt, or Turkey be far behind? Whatever the consequences, Trump's threats to abandon the Iran deal raise the stakes toward nuclear proliferation in the region and the possibility of nuclear war. A far better course would be to resist Israeli paranoia about Iran launching a nuclear attack on Jerusalem (a most unlikely possibility in view of Israel's capacity to retaliate), and allow the nuclear enrichment restrictions to proceed under frequent inspections by the International Atomic Energy Agency.

India and Pakistan

On the Indian subcontinent, a bitter territorial stalemate has existed between India and Pakistan over Kashmir ever since Partition in 1949. Firefights break out from time to time between infantry patrols along the border. Each country has around 110 to 130 nuclear weapons, each with a triad of delivery systems. India's army controls its land-based systems, centered on its Agni I, II, and III intermediate- and long-range missiles. Many of these are MIRVs. The Indian air force provides a secondary strike force of Dassault Mirage 2000 and SEPECAT Jaguar aircraft. The Indian navy has sea-launched ballistic missiles. Pakistan matches all these assets. It has cruise- and intermediate-range missile delivery systems with multiple targeted weapons options. Its missiles are backed up by a secondary air delivery system based on F-16 and JF-17 fighter bombers. It also has a submarine-launch system, which, like India's, is impervious to interdiction. Neither country is a signatory of the nuclear Non-Proliferation Treaty, and thus the nuclear weaponization program of each can freely acquire weapons-grade uranium and reprocessed plutonium from its civil nuclear reactor fleet unimpeded by International Atomic Energy Agency inspections.

A nuclear exchange could occur if either side initiated a first strike. This would not necessarily escalate beyond the subcontinent, because neither country has nuclear allies who would automatically join in. But it would certainly devastate both countries leading to massive loss of life, widespread radioactive contamination, and the possible start of a nuclear winter. A mass exodus of millions of people would be likely. Despite India's refusal to sign on to the Nuclear Non-Proliferation Treaty, the United States during President Obama's watch negotiated a civil nuclear cooperation program with that country. Pakistan now wants a similar deal, but the consensus in Washington has been that this would be unlikely—Pakistan is regarded as too unstable, and American officials have been haunted by the specter of an "Islamic bomb" finding its way from Pakistan into the hands of terrorists. Will Trump's ascendancy make a difference? During a telephone conversation initiated by Prime Minister Nawaz Sharif after Trump's electoral victory, Trump is on record as praising "this amazing country" and offering to do whatever he could to help Pakistan's continued success. But this does not translate into a willingness to negotiate a nuclear cooperation deal similar to the one that the United States has with India.

China

In the South China Sea lie many hundreds of islands and rocky features. Some are claimed and occasionally occupied by Malaysia, Indonesia, Brunei, the Philippines, and Vietnam. A handful of the largest are occupied by China, which is expanding them with dredged sand, airstrips, garrison accommodations, and missile batteries. China claims *all* the islands, but so do the Vietnamese and Taiwanese. Most littoral states are busily expanding their air and naval forces, including submarines. But China deploys an overwhelmingly large maritime fleet comprising fishing boats and coast guard vessels backed up by a rapidly expanding navy. In July 2016, the Philippines won their case against China before the Permanent Court of Arbitration in The Hague over the Scarborough Shoal and features in the Spratly group of islands. But China does not recognize the court's jurisdiction and ignored the ruling. The United States condemned China but lacks moral force because it has not signed the UN Law of the Sea Convention on which the judgment was based. The situation escalates as different groups hold naval exercises in the vicinity (most recently Russia and China, then Australia, Singapore, Malaysia, New Zealand, and the UK). The U.S. Navy continues to send patrols through the Sea.

The Chinese have said that they could take back all the islands but don't want to start a war. The area is a cockpit of increasing tension between China and the United States. What drives China is the carving up of much of its Pacific coast by European powers in unequal treaties during the nineteenth century, and Japan's invasion in the first half of the twentieth. The Chinese have a visceral determination not to allow a repetition of such indignities, and a sense of pride in China's rapid advance as a world hegemon by the mid-twenty-first century. It is only right, they argue, that as an economic superpower, China should control the shore along its Pacific coast. For its part, the United States enjoys a sense of proprietorship of the same territory, for it was they who defeated Japan in the Pacific war, and who, claiming to be an Asia-Pacific power, continue to enjoy the privilege of an overwhelmingly powerful navy. It is a classic case of tension between an old established power and a newly emerging one. The best solution would be for Washington to recognize that China has rights to patrol its own Pacific seaboard, to scale down regular air and sea surveillance by U.S. aircraft and naval vessels along the coast, and to accept the likelihood that China will do nothing to inhibit "freedom of navigation" along regular South China Sea lanes. If, however, the United States continues to project force in the area, a shooting war that could turn nuclear becomes an increasing possibility. On his record so far, President Trump has done nothing to indicate that he might seek to lower the temperature. On the contrary, by accepting in December 2016 a congratulatory call from President Tsai Ing-wen of Taiwan, he has already broken a long-standing practice to which American administrations have so far adhered under the One-China policy. Beijing said very little about the call at the time, and has not publicly reacted to most of Trump's pronouncements about China, North Korea, and the South China Sea. When President Xi Jinping visited Trump's resort at Mar a Lago in Florida in April 2017, harmony and goodwill prevailed, at least on the surface. Xi's demeanor was not even ruffled when, during the visit, Trump ordered the cruise missile assault on the Syrian airfield at al-Shayrat. Nor did Xi react visibly to Trump's declaration at the same time that the United States sought Chinese cooperation in ending the North Korea nuclear menace, but would resolve the issue alone if it was not forthcoming.

North Korea

The principal source of tension in North Asia is North Korea's growing nuclear capability and the rhetoric from Pyongyang that accompanies it. The 1994 Framework arrangements negotiated between the United States and North Korea and signed on 21 October 1994 envisaged a deal under which two Westinghouse proliferation-resistant 1000 MW pressurized water nuclear power plants would be supplied to North Korea in exchange for abandoning its nuclear weapons program. The deal was brokered by former President Jimmy Carter on behalf of President Clinton, and led to the creation of the Korean Peninsula Energy Development Corporation (KEDO), a consortium created on 15 March 1995 between Japan, South Korea, and the United States to supervise the construction of the reactors, and the supply of bunker oil for electricity generation in North Korea until the reactors were completed. Additional signatories were Australia, New Zealand, Canada, Argentina, Chile, the EU, Poland, the Czech Republic, and Uzbekhistan. Part of the deal was for U.S. nuclear technicians to have access to North Korea's single plutonium-generating reactor at Yongpyon in order to extract and safely store dangerously irradiated fuel rods. The agreement worked for eight years until Senator Jesse Helms, Chair of the United States Senate Foreign Relations Committee, reneged on the arrangements in 2003. He did so because of his extreme right-wing perspective about Communism and his sense that North Korea was a rogue state whose bad behavior must not be rewarded. President George W. Bush backed Helms, and North Korea promptly expelled foreign experts, backed away from its nonproliferation commitments, and restarted its plutonium-generating reactor.

Since then North Korea has conducted five nuclear weapons tests and numerous test flights of short-range and medium-range missiles. It has successfully flight-tested its *Musudan* intermediate-range single-stage missile which has a 2,200-mile range, bringing all of Japan and parts of China and Russia within range. Its KN-14 three-stage missile has a range of 6,200 miles, which can reach parts of the United States and Canada. Its KN-08 three-stage missile, yet to be tested, has a claimed range of 7,200 miles, bringing the whole of continental North America within range.

Three other North Korean developments are equally disturbing. First is the regime's claim to have successfully tested a thermonuclear device (some Western observers are skeptical that it was a genuine fission-fusion weapon). Second is its claim to have miniaturized its nuclear bombs to fit onto its missiles—indeed, a recent photo published in the *Bulletin of the Atomic Scientists* shows Kim Jong-un proudly standing beside a sixty-centimeter silver device, probably a plutonium bomb, and estimated to have the explosive force of twenty kilotons, about the same as the bombs dropped on Hiroshima and Nagasaki. Third, North Korea has apparently successfully launched a ballistic missile (SLBM) from one of its submarines. This would give the country a second-strike capability, allowing it to survive an initial nuclear strike and launch its own missiles at sea in retaliation.

As each of these achievements is revealed, hawkish elements in South Korea and Japan have become increasingly insistent that their countries also develop nuclear weapons and delivery systems. Both have substantial numbers of nuclear power reactors. Japan in particular could quickly nuclearize. It possesses 47.8 tons of separated plutonium and 1.2 tons of highly enriched uranium, plus capable ballistic missiles and miniaturizing technology. Since pressured by the United States not to develop its own enrichment and reprocessing plants, South Korea might take a year or two longer.

The United States has sternly invoked security guarantees it has with both countries to discourage them, but the temperature continues to rise between South and North Korea on the one hand, and Japan and North Korea on the other. Tensions are exacerbated by the Pentagon's insistence on continuing to hold regular joint military exercises with South Korea. These involve beach landings and simulated nuclear air strikes against North Korea. Every time the exercises are held, North Korea issues unrestrained threats of condign punishment, including artillery barrages against Seoul. But the Pentagon won't back down, and Washington continues to impose conditions Pyongyang must meet before the United States will sit down and talk about a peace treaty. (North Korea and UN forces are still technically at war under the 1953 Armistice.)

To complicate the situation, unresolved disputes continue between Japan and China over the Senkaku (Diaoyu) islands, and between Japan and South Korea over Takeshima (Dokdo) Island, all situated in the North Pacific. Taken together, these ongoing disputes create another perilous situation that could, through a miscalculation or deliberate act, lead to a nuclear exchange involving China, North Korea, and the United States.

Trump's earlier call for a less confrontational policy toward Russia was a hopeful sign of possible moderation on his part. But it was contradicted by his subsequent declarations, made before and after his election, that he wanted "battlefield nuclear weapons." He seemed not to understand or remember that the practicality of such tactical nuclear weapons was comprehensively rejected by American commanders during nuclear warfare experiments in the 1950s and 1960s. Nor has he shown any inclination toward favoring nuclear disarmament. Although Ronald Reagan espoused aggressive Cold War policies before being elected in 1981, he eventually surprised us with more moderate policies including a near-accommodation with Mikhail Gorbachev at the 1987 Reykjavik Summit to abandon nuclear weapons altogether. This did not eventuate, but it did lead to signing the Intermediate Range Nuclear Forces Agreement in December of the same year. We should not leap to premature conclusions about Trump and should continue to hope that, in his iconoclastic way, he may even come up with solutions that will reduce world tensions. He has at least demonstrated his contempt for accepted assumptions about aggressive Russian behavior (although, regrettably, not about Chinese behavior). Perhaps he will surprise us. Perhaps Trump's commercial sense will intervene to steer him away from reckless behavior. After all, a nuclear exchange with either Russia or China would be very bad for business.

13

Nuclear Weapons: How Foreign Hotspots Could Test Trump's Finger on the Trigger

Julian Borger

On Donald Trump's first day in office he will be handed the "nuclear biscuit"—a small card with the codes he would need to talk to the Pentagon war room to verify his identity in the event of a national security crisis.

Some presidents have chosen to keep the "biscuit" on them, though that is not foolproof. Jimmy Carter left his in his clothes when he sent them to the dry cleaners. Bill Clinton had it in his wallet with his credit cards, but then lost the wallet.

Others have chosen to give the card to an aide to keep in a briefcase, known as the "nuclear football," together with a manual containing U.S. war plans for different contingencies and one on "continuity of government," where to go to ensure executive authority survives a first nuclear strike.

The "biscuit" and "football" are the embodiment of the awesome, civilisation-ending power that will be put in Trump's hands on 20 January. They only become relevant in very rare moments of extreme crisis, but a U.S. president's ability to manage crises around the world will help determine whether they become extreme.

There is one such situation already in the in-tray Trump will find on his desk, on the Korean peninsula, where the North Korean regime is rapidly developing a long-range nuclear missile. Another could blow up at any time with Russia, whose warplanes are flying increasingly close to NATO planes and ships in a high-stakes game of chicken.[1] And Trump could trigger a third crisis, with Iran, if he follows through with his threat to tear up last year's agreement curbing its nuclear programme in return for sanctions relief.

Trump's election has added a new layer of uncertainty to all these potential flash points.

"I have no idea what he would do, and neither, I suspect, does he," said James Acton, the co-director of the nuclear policy programme at the Carnegie Endowment for International Peace. "Let's not kid ourselves he has policies for these issues. He doesn't have a team that has done deep dives into these questions."

The Temperament Question

During the campaign, 10 former U.S. nuclear launch officers, who once manned missile silos and held the keys necessary to execute a launch order, signed a letter saying Trump should not have his "finger on the button" because of his temperament.[2]

One of those former officers, Bruce Blair, said that if U.S. early warning radar showed the country was under attack by nuclear missiles, there would be time for a president to receive a briefing that could be as short as 30 seconds and the commander-in-chief would then have between three and 12 minutes to make up his mind. He would have to take into account that the early warning system had been wrong before and could be vulnerable to ever more sophisticated hacking.

"I think [Trump] lacks knowledge of the world, and knowledge of nuclear weapons and the consequences of their use. He's not competent. He lashes out at the smallest provocation and he divides the world into winners and losers," Blair said. "He's a bully and I wouldn't have confidence that he would be reasoned and restrained in a crisis."

Others have argued that in reality, the decision time is not that short. The fact that the U.S. has so many options—land- and sea-based missiles as well as bombers—means it does not have to launch on warning of an attack. There would be more time for Trump to think and ask for advice.

"The prompt launch of our nuclear missiles is not required nor is it U.S. policy," Peter Huessy, president of Geostrategic Analysis and a guest lecturer at the U.S. Naval Academy, argued.[3]

Kim Jong-un has accelerated testing of nuclear weapons and missiles, and most analysts believe he will reach the capability of making a miniaturised warhead that could be put on an intercontinental ballistic missile capable of reaching the U.S. west coast within Trump's first term as president.

Daryl Kimball, the executive director of the Arms Control Association, said that Pyongyang could seize the opportunity of presidential transition to test Trump's mettle.

"I am worried about the people Trump is going to put in charge on that file," Kimball said. "He is facing a very empty bench. Many of the Republican foreign policy establishment are 'never-Trumpers,' and the North Korea problem is not going to wait."[4]

Trump has offered to talk to Kim, offering the possibility of breaking through the diplomatic impasse that has cut off almost all engagement with the regime.[5] But a unilateral move could unnerve U.S. allies in the region, already anxious about Trump's remarks during the campaign suggesting they do not contribute enough to deserve the shelter of the U.S. nuclear umbrella.[6]

"He has talked about NATO and our alliances with South Korea and Japan as though they are protection rackets," Jeffrey Lewis, director of the East Asia Nonproliferation Programme at the Middlebury Institute of International Studies at Monterey, said. "This is particularly dangerous in South Korea, where there is a significant group of people who think Seoul should be more independent of Washington and acquire nuclear weapons. Asked about Japan or South Korea building nuclear weapons, Trump said 'have a good time.' Japan probably won't take him up on the offer, but South Korea might. I worry South Korea might be followed by Taiwan."

Iran

Trump has threatened to tear up the nuclear deal six major powers signed with Iran last year, in which Iran scaled down its nuclear program in return for relief from international sanctions.[7] He and other Republicans have argued that the U.S. would get more concessions if they reapplied sanctions.

"That would be a catastrophic decision," Acton said. "The other parties to this deal would still consider themselves bound by it, whether or not the U.S. did. If we withdrew, the Iranians would demand redress, and the other parties would be sympathetic. If you want to put pressure on Iran you need multilateral sanctions. Behaving unilaterally is very unlikely to work."

Even before taking office, Trump would be under heavy pressure from the other parties to the deal—the UK, France, Germany, Russia, and China—who have started investing and trading with Iran, not to deliver on his threat.

Doing so could isolate the U.S. and potentially trigger a nuclear arms race in the Gulf.

Russia

Trump has claimed he could improve relations with Russia, and in particular with Vladimir Putin personally, that would defuse the high tensions over Ukraine and Syria. Such deals could well be at the expense of the people of those countries, but could conceivably lessen the chances of a complete end to arms control and the return to an expensive and dangerous nuclear arms race. Hans Kristensen, a nuclear expert at the Federation of American Scientists (FAS), points out that the deepest cuts in nuclear arsenals have been achieved by Republican administrations.

"Republicans love nuclear weapons reductions, as long as they're not proposed by a Democratic president," Kristensen wrote on an FAS blog.[8]

"That is the lesson from decades of U.S. nuclear weapons and arms control management. If that trend continues, then we can expect the new Donald Trump administration to reduce the U.S. nuclear weapons arsenal more than the Obama administration did."[9]

The current arms treaty limiting the strategic arsenals of both countries, New START, expires in 2021. A decision will have to be made whether to replace it or let arms control wither. Both Putin and Trump could save tens of billions of dollars by cutting arsenals. As part of any deal, however, Putin would ask for the scrapping of the U.S. missile defence system currently being erected in eastern Europe. Any concessions on the U.S. trillion-dollar nuclear weapon modernisation programme, which Trump endorses in his transition website, would bring him in direct conflict with the Republican establishment.[10]

"I could imagine Trump personally being more flexible," Acton said. "But it would set up a huge fight with Congress. Congress loves missile defense."

14

The Existential Madness of
Putin-Bashing

Robert Parry

Whatever positive legacy that President Barack Obama might point to—the first African American president, the Affordable Care Act, the changed social attitudes on gay rights, etc.—his ultimate legacy may be defined more by his reckless stewardship guiding the United States into a wholly unnecessary new Cold War. The costs of this Cold War II will be vast, emptying out what's left of the U.S. Treasury in a new arms race against Russia, assuming that the new East-West showdown doesn't precipitate a nuclear war that could end all life on the planet. Already, the U.S. military has altered its national security policies to treat Russia as the principal foreign threat.

"If you want to talk about a nation that could pose an existential threat to the United States, I'd have to point to Russia," said General Joseph F. Dunford Jr., at Senate hearings in 2015 on his nomination to be the new chairman of the Joint Chiefs of Staff. "And if you look at their [the Russians'] behavior, it's nothing short of alarming."[1]

Dunford also recommended shipping U.S. weapons to the post-coup regime in Ukraine so it can better prosecute its war against ethnic Russian rebels in the East who have resisted the overthrow of elected president Viktor Yanukovych and have been deemed "terrorists" by the U.S.-backed government in Kiev.

"Frankly," Dunford said in July 2015, "without that kind of support, they [the new regime in Ukraine] are not going to be able to defend themselves against Russian aggression."[2] Which may prove that no one in official Washington grasps the concept of irony anymore. While Dunford sticks to the propaganda line about "Russian aggression" and the Kiev regime wages its "antiterror operation" against the ethnic Russians in the East, we now know that Kiev has dispatched a military force spearheaded by neo-Nazis and Islamic jihadists with links to Islamic State terrorists.

So, if you want to talk about "aggression" and "terrorism," you might start with the inconvenient truth that the U.S.-beloved government of Ukraine, which supposedly "shares our values," is the first European state since World War II to dispatch Nazi storm troopers to kill other Europeans, and arguably the first ever to create a combined military force of Nazis and Islamic militants (described as "brothers" of the Islamic State).[3]

Yet, when Russia helps these endangered ethnic Russians, who saw their elected president illegally ousted from office in a coup supported, if not sponsored, by the United States, that's "Russian aggression." And, when the ethnic Russians resist the new order, which has now sent Nazis and jihadists to kill them, it's the ethnic Russians who are the "terrorists."

To push the irony even further, while Dunford decried "Russian aggression" in connection with a civil war on Russia's border, he openly declared that the U.S. military stands ready to bomb Iran—halfway around the world—to destroy its nuclear facilities. Asked if the U.S. military had that ability, Dunford said, "My understanding is that we do, Senator."[4]

An Up-Is-Down World

In the up-is-down world that is now official Washington, such extraordinary and profoundly dangerous statements draw only nodding approval from all the important people. In part, that's because President Obama has allowed so many false narratives to take hold regarding Russia, Iran, and other nations, that there is a Grimm's fairy-tale quality to it all.

But the most serious false narrative today is the one about "Russian aggression." Whatever one thinks of Russian president Vladimir Putin, he did not initiate the Ukraine crisis; he reacted to a provocation by neoconservatives in the U.S. government, especially Assistant Secretary of State for European Affairs Victoria Nuland, who sought a "regime change" on Russia's border.

And, while there's plenty of evidence to support the fact that the United States intervened in Ukraine, there is no evidence that Putin sought out this crisis or had any designs to re-create the Russian Empire—two key elements of the U.S. propaganda campaign. The truth is that by encouraging and instigating the violent Ukraine coup on February 22, 2014, the Obama administration struck first.

Putin, who had been preoccupied with the Sochi Winter Olympics at the time, was caught off guard and responded with an emergency national security meeting on February 23 to decide on what steps were needed to protect the Russian strategic interests in Crimea, including the historic naval base at Sevastopol. He was reacting, not instigating.

It may be that President Obama was also surprised by the political crisis in Ukraine, since he also was preoccupied by a variety of other international hotspots, especially in the Middle East. Possibly, he and Secretary of State John Kerry had given too much leeway to Nuland to press for the destabilization of the Yanukovych government.

Nuland, the wife of arch-neocon Robert Kagan, who famously promoted "regime change" in Iraq as a founder of the Project for the New American Century, pushed the envelope in Ukraine in the cause of achieving her own "regime change." Nuland even passed out cookies to antigovernment protesters in Kiev's Maidan Square in fall 2013. In December 2013, Nuland reminded a group of Ukrainian business leaders that the United States had invested $5 billion in their "European aspirations."[5] Then, in early February 2014, Nuland was caught in a precoup phone call with U.S. Ambassador Geoffrey Pyatt discussing which Ukrainian politicians should be elevated in the new government. "Yats is the guy," Nuland said, referring to Arseniy Yatsenyuk, who indeed would become the postcoup prime minister. Dismissing the less aggressive European Union approach to the crisis, Nuland exclaimed, "Fuck the EU!" and pondered how to "glue this thing." Pyatt wondered how to "midwife this thing."[6]

The reality of what happened in Ukraine was never hard to figure out. It was a coup with President Yanukovych forced to flee for his life on February 22, 2014, and extraconstitutional steps then used to remove him as the nation's leader, reminiscent of similar U.S.-orchestrated coups in Iran, Guatemala, Haiti, and Honduras.

But the increasingly unprofessional mainstream U.S. news media had already ditched even a pretense of journalistic objectivity. The media stuck white hats on the coup makers and black hats on Yanukovych (and his ally Putin). The word "coup" became virtually forbidden in the U.S. news media along with any reference to the neo-Nazis who spearheaded it.

Any deviation from this "group think" opened one to charges of "Moscow stooge" or "Putin apologist." Yet, a few people still spoke frankly. George Friedman, for instance, the founder of the global intelligence firm Stratfor, described the overthrow of Yanukovych as "the most blatant coup in history."[7]

Why the Coup?

The motive for the coup was also not hard to divine. Forcing Ukraine out of Russia's economic orbit would deliver a powerful blow to Russia and thus undermine popular support for Putin, all the better to build toward another "regime change" in Moscow.

The plan was laid out on September 26, 2013, by National Endowment for Democracy president Carl Gershman, a major neocon paymaster who distributes more than $100 million a year in U.S. taxpayers' money to undermine governments disfavored by the United States—or, in official Washington speak, to engage in "democracy promotion."

On the op-ed page of the *Washington Post*, Gershman called Ukraine "the biggest prize" and an important interim step toward toppling Putin, who "may find himself on the losing end not just in the near abroad but within Russia itself."[8]

It's also important to remember that in 2013 Putin had offended Washington's powerful neocons by working with President Obama to avert a U.S. military strike against Syria over the mysterious sarin gas attack on August 21, 2013, and by helping to bring Iran to the negotiating table over its nuclear program. In both cases, the neocons wanted to bomb those countries to provoke more "regime change."

So, Putin's peacemaking, and especially his cooperation with Obama to reduce international tensions, made him the new target. Ukraine, with its neuralgic sensitivity for Russians as the historic route for bloody invasions, was the perfect wedge to drive between the two leaders.

Obama could have directed the confrontation in a less hostile direction by insisting on a more balanced presentation of the narrative. He could have recognized that the violent right-wing coup in Kiev provoked an understandable desire among the ethnic Russians of Crimea to secede from Ukraine, a sentiment reflected in the 96 percent vote in a referendum. The ethnic Russians in south and east Ukraine also had reason to fear the extreme Ukrainian nationalists in Kiev.

Instead, Obama bowed to the neocon storyline and bought into the rhetoric about a "Russian invasion." Obama also could have told the American people that there was no credible intelligence suggesting that Putin had aggressive designs on Eastern Europe. He could have tamped down the hysteria, but instead he helped fuel the frenzy.

Before long, the full firepower of the U.S. propaganda arsenal was blasting away, enflaming a new Cold War. That effort was bolstered by the U.S. government pouring tens of millions of dollars into propaganda outlets, often disguised as "bloggers" or "citizen journalists." The U.S. Agency for International Development alone estimates its budget for "media strengthening programs in over 30 countries" at $40 million annually.[9]

USAID, working with billionaire George Soros's Open Society, also funds the Organized Crime and Corruption Reporting Project, which engages in "investigative journalism" that usually goes after governments that have fallen into disfavor with the United States and then are singled out for accusations of corruption. The USAID-funded OCCRP also collaborates with Bellingcat, an online investigative website founded by blogger Eliot Higgins.[10]

Higgins has spread misinformation on the Internet, including discredited claims implicating the Syrian government in the sarin attack in 2013 and directing an Australian TV news crew to what was clearly the wrong location for a video of a Buk antiaircraft battery as it supposedly made its getaway to Russia after the shootdown of Malaysia Airlines Flight 17 in 2014.[11]

Leveling with Americans

Obama could have neutralized much of this propaganda by revealing details about what U.S. intelligence agencies know about some of these pivotal events, but instead he withheld any information that undercuts the preferred propaganda theme.

By staying silent on key questions and preventing the U.S. intelligence community from telling the public what it knows, Obama protected the earlier narratives that put the ethnic Russians and Moscow in the worst possible light. That propaganda has fed the fires of a new Cold War and exacerbated dangerous tensions between the two biggest nuclear powers.

Obama, in his final months in office, could have changed course and leveled with the American people. Instead, he and his intelligence chiefs escalated tensions with Russia by promoting claims that Russia conspired to defeat Hillary Clinton and to put Donald Trump in the White House. The so-called Russia-gate scandal torpedoed Trump's hopes for a more cooperative relationship with Moscow. By the end of his first few months in office, Trump and his national security team were denouncing Russia in terms that might have been expected from a Hillary Clinton. Thus, tensions continued to rise and—given Trump's thin skin and shallow appreciation of geopolitics—the risk of a nuclear war, an extermination event for human civilization, grew worse.

15

Unthinkable? The German Proliferation Debate

Ulrich Kühn

While the United States is still coming to terms with President Donald Trump's domestic and foreign policy, U.S. allies worldwide are becoming increasingly nervous about the new administration's stance toward U.S. alliance commitments. Spurred by Trump's warm words for Russian president Vladimir Putin, his implicit threat that Washington could scale back U.S. defense commitments to Europe if NATO members do not pay more for their own security, and his lax remarks that certain U.S. allies should perhaps be allowed to go nuclear, some prominent voices in Germany are suddenly openly flirting with the nuclear option.[1]

Given the country's long-term support of nuclear disarmament, a debate about a possible German nuclear deterrent is virtually unprecedented. So far, these voices represent an extreme minority view—currently, neither the government nor the vast majority of German experts is even considering the possibility of acquiring nuclear weapons—but with continued uncertainty about Trump's commitment to Europe, this could change during the coming years.

The Pro-Nuclear Arguments

Just three days before the U.S. elections, an op-ed in Germany's largest left-leaning news outlet, *Spiegel* Online, mused about the possibility of Germany pursuing its own nuclear weapons if NATO were to break up in the aftermath of a Trump administration's withdrawal from the alliance.[2]

Two weeks later, Reuters quoted Roderich Kiesewetter, a senior member of Chancellor Angela Merkel's Christian Democratic Union and a high-ranking member of the Bundestag (national parliament), saying that "if the United States no longer wants to provide this [nuclear] guarantee, Europe still needs nuclear protection for deterrent purposes."[3] Given Trump's earlier statements, Kiesewetter continued, "Europe must start planning for its own security in case the Americans sharply raise the cost of defending the continent, or if they decide to leave completely." His suggestion: a Franco-British nuclear umbrella for Europe, financed through a joint European military budget. Under such a scheme, Germany would have to contribute a large amount to the overall costs of such a European deterrent. Further clarifying his remarks, Kiesewetter later pointed out that Europe does not need additional nuclear powers.[4]

On November 28, Germany's most influential conservative newspaper, the *Frankfurter Allgemeine Zeitung*, opened with an op-ed by one of its publishers, Berthold Kohler, preparing Germans for "the unthinkable."[5] Continued Russian and Chinese attempts to expand their spheres of influence, coupled with a possible retreat of the United States, would amount to a "continental shift," the author argued. According to Kohler, the stern implications for Berlin, which for many years relied on the approach of *"Frieden schaffen ohne Waffen"* ("build peace without weapons"), would be obvious: if Germany wants to successfully bargain with the Kremlin, he implies, it has to be able to credibly defend its allies (which is an interesting hint at the changed power relations in Europe). Kohler concludes that this could mean increased defense spending, a return to conscription, the drawing of red lines, and an indigenous nuclear deterrent. He is quick to insinuate that the French and British arsenals are currently "too weak" to take on Russia and China.

The Two Paths

Even though these remarks and op-eds do not build or comment on each other, they begin to reveal contours of a debate. One can see two paths of proposed action if the United States were to withdraw or openly question its security guarantees: a European nuclear option and a German nuclear option.

Following Kiesewetter's suggestions, a potential European nuclear option could be interpreted as an extreme, though not logically conclusive, part of a larger ongoing effort to give the European Union more credible and integrated defense structures.[6] German minister of defense Ursula von der Leyen is already lobbying for a bigger EU global security role and higher defense spending.[7] There is little doubt that these efforts are also a reaction to Trump's campaign comments. But more so, they represent a change in German foreign and security policy dating to 2013, when President Joachim Gauck cautioned Germans that "in a world full of crises and upheaval, Germany has to take on new responsibilities."[8]

In contrast, a potential indigenous German nuclear option is by no means grounded in or linked to any ongoing political debate about Germany's role as a security provider for Europe. Nevertheless, it is indeed a reflection—though an extreme and perhaps hysterical one—of the multiple crises and threats Europe is facing. These include, inter alia, an increasingly aggressive and militaristic Russia, the war in eastern Ukraine, the British Brexit vote, the war in Syria and the related refugee crises, and the heavy-handed authoritarian rule of President Recep Tayyip Erdoğan in Turkey.

Against this background, certain segments of the German strategic community seem deeply concerned about the uncertain effects of four (or eight) years of U.S. foreign and security policy under Trump. Not completely without reason, their criticism of him points to the fact that extended nuclear deterrence rests on a fragile, psychological bargain between the provider (the United States), the recipient (the NATO allies), and the addressee (Russia), which can only be upheld if all sides believe to a certain degree in the credibility of the deterring threat. Trump's questioning of the continuity of U.S. security commitments places the whole bargain under stress. In this context, musing about a German deterrent could be interpreted as nuclear signaling to both Washington and Moscow.

The Current Realities

Notwithstanding the recent public airing of nuclear flirtations, powerful and convincing arguments speak against a German or non-NATO European nuclear option. All things nuclear are highly unpopular among ordinary Germans. In a recent poll, 85 percent of Germans spoke against the continued deployment of U.S. nuclear weapons in Germany.[9] More than 90 percent approved the idea of an international ban on nuclear weapons.[10] Even among policy makers, nuclear weapons policies have always been dealt with in a cautious and sometimes skeptical way. The 2009 coalition contract of Merkel's ruling conservative party, for instance, held out the prospect of Germany working within NATO on a full withdrawal of U.S. nuclear weapons from German soil.[11]

But since the Russian annexation of Crimea, the German government has been fully supportive of NATO's nuclear-sharing arrangements and opposes the latest push in the United Nations toward a nuclear weapons ban treaty.[12] Musings about a European deterrent, as articulated by Kiesewetter, would run counter to German efforts to remind the Trump administration of the value of NATO's Article 5 commitments and the U.S. role as a security provider for Europe. In fact, they could give Trump carte blanche to argue that if Europe were to have its own deterrent, then why would it need Washington's guarantees? It is also not clear how a Franco-British deterrent for Europe could take shape with London currently exiting from the European project.

In addition, Berlin just announced an increase in its defense spending by 8 percent in 2017, taking defense expenditures to

1.22 percent of its GDP.[13] This is a significant increase, even though Germany remains considerably below its NATO commitment of spending at least 2 percent of its GDP on defense. Nevertheless, Germany can point to its efforts in the upcoming consultations with the new Trump team to counter criticism about its defense commitments to NATO. A possible German nuclear option would only distract from the core message that Germany is ready to take on more responsibility within the alliance and Europe as a whole.

Even if Germany was to attempt to go nuclear, the hurdles would be extremely high. Although the country is one of the most technically advanced nations in the world and it theoretically possesses enough fissile material for a nuclear device, the enormous financial and political costs that would come with such a decision would most likely outweigh any perceived benefit.[14]

There are also many political-legal obstacles. Germany would have to withdraw from or seek to change the 1990 Treaty on the Final Settlement with Respect to Germany (also known as the Two Plus Four Treaty), which it signed together with France, the Soviet Union, the United Kingdom, and the United States.[15] In that agreement, the reunified Germany reaffirmed its "renunciation of the manufacture and possession of and control over nuclear, biological, and chemical weapons." In addition, Berlin would openly violate commitments under the international Treaty on the Non-Proliferation of Nuclear Weapons, the International Atomic Energy Agency, and the European Atomic Energy Community.

From Fringe to Mainstream

Obviously, current German nuclear flirtations represent a fringe view, but they are an important early warning sign. These flirtations were carried by Germany's biggest left-leaning and conservative media outlets. In addition, Kiesewetter is not a backbencher or low-ranking politician from a small party. As a former *Bundeswehr* (armed forces) general staff officer; former chairman of the Subcommittee for Disarmament, Arms Control and Non-Proliferation of the Bundestag; and current spokesperson of the Committee on Foreign Affairs, he is well-versed in foreign and security policy matters. That a person of his stature would raise such a view is reason enough for concern.

Further, extreme views on nuclear matters do not always remain at the fringes. As the case of South Korea demonstrates, external shocks such as the repeated nuclear tests by North Korea in 2013 can quickly move formerly fringe positions to the center stage of public attention.[16] Once in the mainstream, it can be difficult to put such sentiments to rest, particularly when the underlying security concerns remain.

To be clear, the Merkel administration is far from considering a European or German nuclear option, and other major political parties on the left are traditionally strong opponents of a more muscular nuclear weapons approach. For example, Rainer Arnold, defense spokesman for the ruling coalition partner of the Social Democrats in parliament, was quick to dismiss Kiesewetter's suggestion as "off base."[17] In fact, for decades, Berlin acted as a staunch advocate of nuclear disarmament and nonproliferation policies, and isolated instances of German proliferation signaling were extremely rare.[18] But their now sudden and unexpected occurrence is telling with regard to the devastating effects of Trump's loose and uninformed talk about U.S. alliance commitments and long-standing American nonproliferation policies.

Beyond those more narrow observations, the "Trump shock" and its effects—which caught most German policy makers off guard—point to U.S. allies' wider concerns about America's role in the world and the likely period of unpredictability and volatility ahead. Underlying these perceptions and developments are strategic discontinuities that can occur quite rapidly and result in previously unimaginable developments. A U.S. retreat from long-held global political and normative positions would be such a sudden discontinuity. Germany's final acceptance of the role of a benevolent hegemon in Europe, in combination with the British retreat, would be another. Combined, they could give rise to alternative policy concepts and cognitive adjustments. The current German nuclear flirtation is just one, and certainly not the last, sign of the changing European security landscape.

PART THREE

NUCLEAR REMEDIES

16

Law and Morality at the Vienna Conference on the Humanitarian Impact of Nuclear Weapons

Ray Acheson

Law stands on hollow ground where a solid moral conviction is absent. On the contrary, a gap in law is often just a mirror through which we are impelled to gaze into our own ambivalent souls. And so it is the case with nuclear weapons.

—Dr. Nobuo Hayashi, University of Oslo

The Vienna conference on the humanitarian impact of nuclear weapons, hosted by Austria in December 2014, was the third in a series of international meetings that set out to illuminate and refine our understanding of the devastating effects of nuclear weapons. But it went beyond earlier meetings to articulate a commitment to a specific political response to this challenge: the stigmatization, prohibition, and elimination of nuclear weapons. By mid-2015 this commitment had been transformed into a Humanitarian Pledge. So far, it has been endorsed by 127 states.[1] This common pledge laid the groundwork for committed states to pursue measures for nuclear disarmament even without the participation of nuclear-armed states. It set the stage for the UN General Assembly to adopt a resolution in October 2016 establishing negotiations in 2017 on a legally binding instrument to prohibit nuclear weapons. The first round of these negotiations was held in New York from March 27 through 31, 2017; the second round will be held from June 15 through July 7, 2017.

The Humanitarian Conferences

The series of conferences on the humanitarian impact of nuclear weapons collectively provided irrefutable evidence about the devastating consequences and risks of the use of nuclear weapons. They also gave voice to international organizations and UN agencies, which have emphatically reported that they would not be able to effectively respond to the use of nuclear weapons.[2]

The Vienna conference added new dimensions, including survivor testimonies from testing victims, a closer examination of risks, and most important, an exploration of the moral, normative, and legal frameworks governing nuclear weapons.[3]

Ethics, Morality, and the Failure of Nuclear Deterrence

In his presentation during the final panel at the Vienna conference, Nobuo Hayashi from the University of Oslo noted that the law does not address the legality of nuclear weapons in the way it does biological and chemical weapons. "It is as though we can strangulate this beast from all directions, but not quite strike directly at its heart."[4]

Some governments have repeatedly questioned this distinction among the weapons of mass destruction. At the Vienna conference, the Irish delegation asked, Why should nuclear weapons be viewed as somehow more "necessary," "legitimate," or "justifiable" than other weapons of mass destruction? "Is that because of a belief in their value as a deterrent?" asked the Irish delegate. "Then why has this deterrent failed to prevent conflicts breaking out in various regions in which the parties directly or indirectly involved have nuclear weapons in their arsenals?"[5]

Nuclear deterrence took a hit at the Vienna conference, with most states reiterating long-held views that nuclear weapons bring insecurity and instability, not safety and protection. Only a handful of states argued that nuclear weapons provide some "security bene-fit" that must be taken into account when considering legal or policy options. Yet despite the consistent and overwhelming objections to the concept and practice of nuclear deterrence, human society has still failed to establish law prohibiting and setting out a framework for the elimination of nuclear weapons the same way it has for bio-logical and chemical weapons. Why?

It is not because nuclear weapons have some sort of inherent, magical value that other weapons of mass destruction do not have. It has much more to do with the way nuclear weapons are positioned within the political-military-academic-industrial nexus than any-thing else. Any "magic" these weapons are perceived to possess has been falsely granted to them by those who benefit from them mate-rially or politically. But like all magic, the illusion can be unmasked and its power taken away.

An important step in unveiling the truth about nuclear weapons could be through unleashing our "moral imagination." Dr. Hayashi suggested that we have been imprisoned by arguments for or against nuclear weapons that are built on an "ethics of outcome." That is, we tend to look at the consequences of the use of nuclear weapons and decide whether or not the ends justify the means. Instead, we might start looking at the suffering nuclear weapons cause as "suf-fering per se, rather than suffering that is necessary or unnecessary for this or that purpose."[6]

He drew upon the shift in thinking about torture as a precedent for this approach, arguing that "most of us now agree that torture is a moral wrong in itself, and that under no circumstances do outcome-based claims ever justify it."[7] Fittingly, the CIA torture report was released in the United States the same day Dr. Hayashi gave his presentation in Vienna. The massive outcry in the United States and beyond indicates that despite continued justifications by certain people, the findings have been condemned as abhorrent and unacceptable by the majority of the world. Would the reaction be the same if nuclear weapons were to be used again today? While the users might claim they had the right and the responsibility to wreak the havoc and devastation promised by nuclear weapons, would the rest of the world really accept it?

Lithuania's delegation remarked that the testimonies of survivors have become a powerful moral deterrent against any use of nuclear weapons. The voices of survivors from Australia, Japan, Kazakhstan, the Marshall Islands, and the United States at the Vienna conference indeed could not be denied. Even the U.S. delegation, after a rather callous delay, thanked those who brought personal testimonies to the conference.

But will these voices deter use? Can they deter the threat of use? Can they deter possession?

If we cannot conceive of accepting the use of nuclear weapons and the suffering it will bring, how can we accept the ongoing practice of nuclear deterrence? How can we accept that the use of these weapons is written into "security" doctrines of states? That they are deployed, on alert, ready to use? That they still exist, in any hands?

Humanitarian Pledge

At the end of the conference, the Austrian government delivered both a Chair's summary and also a pledge. One of the most important points in the Chair's summary was that the suffering caused by nuclear weapons use necessitates both legal and moral appraisals, and that a comprehensive legal norm universally prohibiting nuclear weapons is currently missing.

The Chair's summary also reflected the views of states conveyed during the general debate, including that many delegations "expressed support for the negotiation of a new legal instrument prohibiting nuclear weapons."[8]

Austria also presented a pledge at the end of the conference, which highlights the conviction that efforts are needed to stigmatize, prohibit, and eliminate nuclear weapons and says that Austria will pursue measures to "fill the legal gap" for prohibiting and eliminating nuclear weapons.[9] After the conference, Austria welcomed other states to join them in this pledge. By April 2016, 127 states had done so. The pledge was also introduced as a resolution in the UN General Assembly in December 2015; 139 states voted in favor of its adoption.[10]

Filling the Legal Gap

The International Campaign to Abolish Nuclear Weapons (ICAN), a civil society coalition of over 400 organizations in 100 countries, believes that in the current context the best way to fill the legal gap is with a treaty banning nuclear weapons. Such a treaty can be negotiated now, even without the participation of the nuclear-armed states if they choose not to join. A nuclear weapon ban treaty would formalize the global rejection of nuclear weapons by prohibiting their possession, use, storage, sharing, transfer, and development. The ban treaty itself need not necessarily envisage every complex step toward elimination by all states. Instead it would put in place the basic framework for reaching that goal.[11]

Underpinning this strategy is a firm belief that changing the legal, political, and financial landscape of nuclear weapons would have a significant impact beyond those states that may formally adopt such an instrument at the outset. "The ban treaty, once in force, would powerfully challenge any notion that possessing nuclear weapons is legitimate for particular states," ICAN has argued.[12]

But we cannot just fill this gap with law alone. One of the biggest challenges with nuclear weapons is that existing law is being circumvented. If the nuclear Non-Proliferation Treaty were being implemented, we would not have nuclear sharing arrangements, and the nuclear-armed states would be engaged in multilateral negotiations for the elimination of their arsenals. We would also not see billions of dollars flowing toward the modernization of nuclear weapons for decades to come.[13]

To give the law power and resilience we must also fill the gap with morality, compassion, responsibility, and accountability.

Vienna gave us a starting point. It gave us a pledge to pursue a legal prohibition on nuclear weapons. But it also gave us a way forward in reconstructing how we think about and approach nuclear weapons.

From Pledge to Action

At the Vienna conference, the overwhelming majority of governments condemned the possession of nuclear weapons and insisted that they must never be used again under any circumstances. Less than two years later, sixty-eight states voted in favor of a UN working group report recommending that the UN General Assembly commence negotiations in 2017 on a legally binding treaty to prohibit nuclear weapons, leading to their elimination.[14] At least 107 states indicated their support for this recommendation during the course of the open-ended working group on taking forward multilateral nuclear disarmament negotiations, which met in February, May, and August 2016.[15] This was an historic moment, the "most significant contribution to nuclear disarmament in two decades," as the Mexican delegation said in its closing remarks to the meeting.

Subsequently, on October 27, 2016, the General Assembly adopted a resolution establishing negotiations to take place in March and June/July 2017; 123 states voted in favor of the resolution, standing up to the opposition of the nuclear-armed states and many of their nuclear-supportive allies. These negotiations began on March 27. The first week was a resounding success, with 132 states, international organizations, and civil society actively participating. Based on the debates held during this first round of talks, there is clearly broad agreement on most of the core prohibitions as well as the principles and objectives of the treaty. Outstanding issues include whether or not the treaty should prohibit threat of use, testing, and financing; how to best address victim and survivor rights and environmental remediation; and how to deal with stockpiling and verification. In the weeks ahead, it will be important for governments and civil society groups to work together to solve these remaining issues. The president of the conference, Ambassador Elayne Whyte Gómez of Costa Rica, will prepare a draft text of the treaty, to be circulated to participating states in the latter half of May or early June. Negotiations will resume at the UN for three weeks starting on June 15, during which time governments will work their way through the draft with the aim of concluding the treaty by July 7.

The battle is far from over. It is understood that achieving the elimination of nuclear weapons will take more than a prohibition treaty on its own, and it is widely anticipated that some states will continue to try to thwart progress during negotiations of the ban treaty. The U.S. government has already called on all states "to reject unrealistic efforts to ban nuclear weapons" and instructed its NATO allies to not participate in the negotiations.[16] The Trump administration also led a press conference outside of the conference room on the first day of negotiations to protest the world moving ahead to prohibit nuclear weapons. Of course, if banning nuclear weapons is so unrealistic, the United States should have nothing to fear. But the United States and the other nuclear-armed states and some of their allies that purport to receive protective value from nuclear weapons are actively opposing ban treaty efforts, signaling their awareness of the practical, normative, legal, political, economic, and social effects such a treaty will have on their continued support for nuclear weapons.

For seventy-one years the majority of countries have experienced the injustice and insecurity that nuclear weapons represent. The scene looks different now. Committed states and civil society have launched a concerted, credible challenge to nuclear weapons. They have the momentum and the moral authority to succeed.

17

A New Movement to Ban Nuclear Weapons

Tim Wright

In 2007 a group of Australians launched the International Campaign to Abolish Nuclear Weapons—ICAN—in an effort to reignite the languishing global antinuclear movement, to get better organized, and to finish the work of decades past. It was an ambitious undertaking, but we felt confident then, and feel confident now, that it is a battle we will ultimately win. In many ways, we are *already* succeeding.

This might seem a naïve claim in light of all we know about the precarious state of the planet—the thousands of nuclear warheads on hair-trigger alert, and the numerous barriers to nuclear disarmament. But there is good cause for optimism. Over the past few years, we have seen the start of a fundamental shift in the way that governments talk about nuclear weapons—not the governments of nuclear-armed nations or their nuclear-weapon-supporting allies, who remain firmly stuck in Cold War thinking, but the rest: the 150 or so nonnuclear nations, who constitute an overwhelming majority.

Possessing the bomb is not the norm. Almost every nation in the world has made a legal undertaking never to acquire nuclear weapons. For years, these nations have taken a backseat in disarmament debates, feeling powerless to act, hoping idly that the promises of nuclear-armed states would someday be fulfilled. But no longer: a new humanitarian-focused initiative for nuclear disarmament has emerged because of mounting frustration at the failure of

nuclear-armed states to fulfill their decades-old disarmament commitments. It has emerged out of recognition that simply bemoan-
ing inaction, no matter how loudly, is not an effective strategy for
achieving abolition. Why would one expect the nuclear-armed
states to lead us to a nuclear-weapon-free world? Why would they
willingly give up weapons they hold so dear, that they perceive as
the ultimate guarantor of their security, that they believe afford
them prestige in international affairs?

To draw an analogy with the banning of smoking in public places:
we would never expect the smoking community to initiate and lead
efforts to impose such a ban. We would expect them stridently to
resist it. The nonsmoking majority, who wish to live and work in
a healthy environment, must be the driving force. No one would
question that logic. Similarly, it is the nonnuclear-weapon states
who must drive a process to ban nuclear weapons, to stigmatize
them, make them socially and politically unacceptable, to make it
harder for nations to get away with possessing and upgrading them,
and to *help* the nuclear-weapon states overcome their debilitating
addiction.

This flips the traditional arms-control approach on its head. The
humanitarian-focused approach is about empowering and mobiliz-
ing the rest of the world to say "enough." It is about shifting the
debate from "acceptable," "safe" numbers of nuclear warheads to
their fundamental inhumanity and incompatibility with basic standards of civilized behavior. It is about taking away from the nuclear-
armed states the power to dictate the terms of the debate and set the
agenda—and refusing to perpetuate their exceptionalism.

This new approach to nuclear disarmament began to emerge in
2010. Jakob Kellenberger, then the president of the International
Committee of the Red Cross, delivered an important address to the
Geneva diplomatic corps that April, spelling out his organization's
commitment on humanitarian grounds to "bringing the era of
nuclear weapons to an end."[1] Shortly thereafter, the state parties to
the Non-Proliferation Treaty, at their five-yearly review conference

in May, expressed "deep concern at the catastrophic humanitarian consequences of any use of nuclear weapons."[2]

Additionally, in 2013 and 2014 the governments of Norway, Mexico, and Austria hosted three major intergovernmental conferences to present the irrefutable evidence of the catastrophic immediate and long-term impacts of nuclear detonations, and the inability of relief agencies to provide any meaningful response in the event of a nuclear attack. At the conference in Mexico, held in February 2014, the chair concluded with a call to launch a diplomatic process to negotiate a legally binding instrument prohibiting nuclear weapons.[3] He declared the conference "a point of no return."

At the third humanitarian conference, in Vienna in December 2014, the Austrian government issued a "pledge" to work with all relevant stakeholders, including civil society, the United Nations, and the international Red Cross movement, "to fill the legal gap for the prohibition and elimination of nuclear weapons."[4] It then invited all interested states to endorse the pledge, and 127 did so. In 2016, building on these successes, the UN General Assembly adopted a landmark resolution establishing a formal mandate for negotiations on a treaty prohibiting nuclear weapons. This was not a radical decision: indiscriminate, inhumane weapons get banned. Nuclear weapons are the only "weapons of mass destruction" not yet subject to a comprehensive, global prohibition. The vast majority of nations are committed to rectifying that legal anomaly.

It is worth recalling that, in the 1990s, a small group of humanitarian-minded nations, with the strong encouragement of civil society, decided to initiate a similar diplomatic process to outlaw antipersonnel mines. They began by assembling the evidence of the catastrophic impact that those pernicious devices have on people and the environment. That, they knew, would provide a solid foundation for successful negotiations. And this is what we have seen happen in the nuclear sphere.

Of course, many of the major users and producers of land mines stubbornly refused to participate in negotiations for the Mine Ban

Treaty. They claimed that such weapons were fundamental to their security. U.S. allies such as Australia worked actively to undermine the process, proposing gaping loopholes and voicing skepticism at every opportunity. But the treaty has been successful beyond expectations. Few nations today use or stockpile land mines, whereas their use in the past was widespread. Since the treaty entered into force in 1999, the number of land-mine-related deaths and injuries has dropped by over 60 percent.

We are under no illusion that a treaty banning nuclear weapons will be a panacea. It will not magically transport us to a nuclear-weapon-free world overnight. But it will fundamentally change the game. It offers an alternative to waiting in vain for U.S. and Russian leadership. This is a way to translate into law the tenet propounded by the former UN secretary-general Ban Ki-moon that "there are no right hands for wrong weapons."[5] It would stigmatize nuclear weapons in the same way that chemical and biological weapons have been stigmatized through conventions. Angela Kane, then the secretary-general's high representative for disarmament affairs, asked rhetorically in an address in New Zealand in April 2014: "How many states today boast that they are 'biological-weapon states' or 'chemical-weapon states'? Who is arguing now that bubonic plague or polio are legitimate to use as weapons under any circumstance, whether in an attack or in retaliation? Who speaks of a bio-weapon umbrella?"[6]

Through its normative force, a nuclear weapon ban treaty would profoundly affect the behavior even of states that refuse to join. The public, the media, parliamentarians, and mayors would have a powerful new tool with which to challenge the possession of nuclear weapons by their governments. The ban would compel allies of nuclear-armed states to end the practice of hosting nuclear weapons on their soil, and to reject the pretense of protection from a "nuclear umbrella." It would oblige all states to divest from companies that manufacture nuclear arms.

The Non-Proliferation Treaty falsely divides the world into

nuclear-weapon states and nonnuclear-weapon states. In reality, there is a significant group in the middle: thirty or so nations that claim the protection of U.S. nuclear weapons. These nations reinforce the idea that nuclear weapons are legitimate, useful, and necessary instruments of war. The humanitarian-based disarmament approach has shone a spotlight on these enabler states, known less affectionately as "weasel states," and they are scampering. They are not accustomed to this level of scrutiny. They have always claimed to be committed to disarmament. But clearly they are part of the problem—and *that* we can change.

Many of these governments are vulnerable to public pressure. Japan, despite having experienced the horrors of nuclear war, maintains a policy of reliance on U.S. nuclear weapons. In 2013 the government rejected an invitation by South Africa to sign on to a joint statement declaring that nuclear weapons should never be used again, "under any circumstances."[7] ICAN protested that decision by organizing a small, spontaneous demonstration outside the Japanese permanent mission to the UN in Geneva. It made primetime news in Japan, prompting the foreign minister to convene a press conference to defend the decision, which only intensified the furor. The mayor of Nagasaki, in his annual peace declaration, condemned Japan's stance as a betrayal of the expectations of the world community.[8] And so Japan changed its position.

This is a small example of how we are winning. The joint statement itself was not an especially significant one. It was merely a political declaration, not a legally binding instrument. But the public's ability to influence the Japanese government's position so dramatically, against its wishes and those of the United States, was of enormous significance. And we will see more of this in Japan and elsewhere as the process to achieve a treaty banning nuclear weapons moves forward.

Listening to the debates in the United States in 2010 about whether the Senate should ratify the New START agreement with Russia, I was stuck by the comment of one senator that pursuing nuclear arms reductions is not America's decision alone, for America's allies, too, depend on U.S. nuclear weapons and thus have a stake, and they want the U.S. arsenal to remain strong and large. The wishes of NATO allies and others were, in other words, a reason for maintaining the status quo. But what if that excuse no longer existed? What if these nations were on *our* side, as state parties to a future treaty banning nuclear weapons? That would have profound flow-on effects for civil society's work in the United States to advance disarmament.

The U.S. government, interestingly, felt compelled to attend the Vienna Conference on the Humanitarian Impact of Nuclear Weapons in 2014, having boycotted the earlier two conferences in Norway and Mexico, which it disingenuously labeled a "distraction" from America's many other efforts to achieve nuclear disarmament.[9] Why the apparent change of heart? Was the United States suddenly supportive of this initiative? Not at all—that was obvious in Vienna. But it is largely beside the point—this initiative does not depend on U.S. endorsement. Its success will depend on the collective resolve of nuclear-free nations and effective public mobilization.

In a tone-deaf statement delivered immediately after the searing testimonies of survivors of America's nuclear atrocities in Japan and the Marshall Islands, as well as its own backyard, the U.S. ambassador declared that America does not support, and will oppose, moves to ban nuclear weapons. He came across as callous, almost comically out of touch, a pariah in the room—not the mythical "responsible" nuclear power. The humanitarian initiative has torn that concept apart.

The United States attended Vienna for two reasons: it wanted to be seen as doing the right thing in the minds of its own citizens and before the international community, and it wanted to stop the ban treaty proposal from gaining any further traction. But the momentum of this initiative is already too great. The train has left the station and is gaining speed. Some states will, naturally, get off along the way; others will jump on board. There is no doubt that the journey will be a rocky one. But we are confident that the train will reach its destination. This will require, however, the active and dedicated support of thousands of individuals globally. "If you love this planet," to use Helen Caldicott's words, I encourage you to become part of the International Campaign to Abolish Nuclear Weapons—to work with hundreds of diverse organizations around the world to put in place a global legal prohibition on the worst weapons ever created. More than seven decades have passed since the U.S. atomic bombings of Hiroshima and Nagasaki, which claimed the lives of a quarter of a million innocent civilians. It is well beyond time to begin negotiations on a ban.

18

Don't Bank on the Bomb

Susi Snyder

Nuclear weapons are things that we tend to think of in the abstract. We tend to think that only politicians or government can do anything about them. We tend to think our role is solely to try to influence those who create and implement policy.

Nuclear weapons disempower us.

Nuclear weapons threaten us with destruction, fire, burning, and radiation. In all honesty, they are big and scary bombs that form the stuff of fantasy, or nightmares. But we can actually do something about them. We can act to stigmatize nuclear weapons, leading to their outlaw and elimination.

Most people agree that there is a stigma associated with nuclear weapons—that they are weapons that are not "good." This is why so much attention and support is given to nonproliferation. We know deep down that any use of these weapons would cause catastrophic effects that would not be constrained by borders. The stigma is important—we know nuclear weapons are bad, but now we need to redefine them as unacceptable. Governments are preparing to do so by establishing a United Nations conference to negotiate a legally binding instrument to prohibit nuclear weapons, leading toward their total elimination in 2017.

But civilians can do something too. To get to the root of many problems, one can trace the money. And, when it comes to nuclear weapons, by following the money, we can cut it off. While this isn't the only thing necessary to make nuclear weapons extinct, it will help. And it just may prevent our own extinction along the way.

Taken together, the nine nuclear-armed states are planning to spend more than $1 trillion over the next decade to maintain and modernize their nuclear weapons. That is $66,000 per minute, or about $10,000 more—per minute—than the normal U.S. family earns in a year.

It is important that people know and understand that they have the power to influence the companies profiting from the persistent threat of nuclear annihilation. The majority of the money that will be spent on new nuclear weapons comes from taxpayers in the nuclear-armed countries, but the companies behind the bomb cannot make profits without investment from the private sector. The 2016 *Don't Bank on the Bomb* report shows that 390 banks, pension funds, and asset managers in twenty-six countries made more than $498 billion available between January 2013 and August 2016 to twenty-seven companies that produce, maintain, and modernize nuclear arsenals in France, India, the United Kingdom, and the United States.

Many of the companies involved in the production of nuclear weapons do so for more than one arsenal. For the United States and the United Kingdom, which share technologies related to the Trident DII missile system, this is logical. However, one of the same companies is also involved in the French nuclear arsenal. These companies benefit from the political drive in each of these countries to maintain so-called independent systems, even though the systems themselves may not be as unique as most people think.

A wide range of financial institutions operate in our globalized world. These include privately owned companies and state-owned institutions, banks, insurance companies, investment funds, investment banks, pension funds, export credit agencies, and many others. As a large majority of companies rely on the financial markets and financial institutions to provide them with operating capital, these financial institutions play a key role in every segment of human activity. In choosing which companies and projects they will finance and invest in, financial institutions play a significant role in the world. Choosing to avoid investment in controversial items—from tobacco to nuclear arms—can result in changed global policies, and reduces the chances of humanitarian harm.

Don't Bank on the Bomb reports examine which companies are involved, and what companies have current contracts to maintain and modernize nuclear arsenals. The report identifies twenty-seven nuclear-weapons-producing companies. Some are well known—Lockheed Martin and Raytheon. The involvement of others with nuclear weapons is surprising—like Boeing and Airbus. Some of them are not well known at all, such as Moog. These companies are mostly located in the nuclear-armed countries, but not all. For example, Leonardo-Finmeccanica is an Italian company, and works on the French arsenal. Airbus, which used to be called EADS, is registered in the Netherlands.

These companies are providing what is necessary to develop, test, maintain, and modernize nuclear weapons. The contracts these companies have with nuclear-armed countries are for materials and services to keep nuclear weapons in their arsenals. In other nuclear-armed countries—Russia, China, Pakistan, and North Korea—the maintenance and modernization of nuclear forces is carried out primarily or exclusively by government agencies.

For the private companies, the Don't Bank on the Bomb campaign has developed a Hall of Shame: 390 institutions in some kind of financial relationship with nuclear-weapons producers. These relationships range from bond- or shareholding to investment banking services. Few people are surprised that JPMorgan Chase is an investor, but Cigna? They also have millions invested. State Street, the wealth management agent, is the biggest investor the campaign has identified overall, investing over $27 billion, but State Farm? State Farm has $855 million invested. TIAA-CREF, the teachers' pension plan, has more than $6 billion invested. The New Jersey Department of the Treasury—they hold the pensions for the firefighters and cops (among others)—has $92 million invested. (These are the parent companies, not the subsidiaries. So, for example, Bank of Austria isn't on the list, because it's a subsidiary of UniCredit.)

Most of the people whose pension funds are being invested by these companies probably don't know that their investments support nuclear weapons. There is a tremendous lack of knowledge across financial institutions and their clients about the private-sector connection to nuclear weapons. And it turns out that a lot of financial institutions don't want to have any association with nuclear weapons.

It is important to give credit to those who act on the nuclear weapons stigma, and put their money where their mouth is. Don't Bank on the Bomb has created Hall of Fame and Runners-Up categories to illustrate the art of the possible. Overall, the campaign has found more than fifty financial institutions with policies that prohibit or limit their investments in companies associated with nuclear weapons.

The Hall of Fame financial institutions have the best of the best policies. Currently, research has identified eighteen financial institutions with a public policy that is comprehensive in scope and application. The financial institutions in the Hall of Fame are based in Australia, Denmark, Italy, the Netherlands, Norway, Sweden, and the United Kingdom. By highlighting these financial institutions, the campaign aims to show that institutions can and do decide to ban investments in the nuclear-weapons industry.

The Runners-Up highlights more financial institutions that have taken the step to exclude nuclear-weapons producers from their investments, but whose policy is not all-inclusive in preventing financial involvement with nuclear-weapons companies. The Runners-Up category is quite broad in definition and offers a place to some financial institutions that are almost eligible for the Hall of Fame, but also to some institutions with a policy that contains loopholes that still allow for considerable sums of money to be invested in nuclear-weapons producers. For example, sometimes the institution does not apply the policy to all of their financial products, or they say they will not finance the nuclear-weapons-related projects but provide general corporate funds (even though this frees up capital to be moved into nuclear weapons projects). These policies illuminate the ongoing debates financial institutions are engaged in today.

The campaign then has conversations with the Runners-Up financial institutions. They ask for advice on how to get out of the Hall of Shame, how to move on up to the Hall of Fame. No one wants the stigma associated with nuclear weapons, and between 2014 and 2015 the campaign saw a 50 percent increase in stigmatizing policies.

The policy level is where we can have some serious impact.

Public pressure can change the policies of financial institutions and encourage the development of policies that prohibit any investment in nuclear weapons.

Simply alerting financial institution clients of these investments can change the policies, and lead to divestment from nuclear-weapons producers. Almost every member of the public has a bank account or is part of a pension plan. If your bank or pension fund is investing in nuclear-weapons producers, so are you. Divestment campaigns are a way to bring an abstract issue such as nuclear disarmament back to personal decisions on where people put their own money.

Divestment works.

While it is unlikely that divestment by a single financial institution will create sufficient pressure on a company for it to end its involvement in nuclear-weapons work, divestment by even a few institutions based on the same ethical objection can have a significant impact on a company's strategic direction.

Exclusions by financial institutions have a stigmatizing effect and can convince directors to decide to reduce reliance on nuclear-weapons contracts and expand into other areas.

In the Stop Explosive Investments, the focus is disinvestment from cluster-munitions producers. Granted, cluster munitions, unlike nuclear weapons, have been clearly outlawed through a specific international treaty. Nevertheless, not every country has stopped making cluster bombs, and the divestment campaign has had a clear and significant effect.

Everyone knows that one of the biggest global weapons-producing companies is Lockheed Martin. They work hard to brand themselves as the world's top arms manufacturer. So, it is hard to imagine that Lockheed Martin would listen or stop making weapons. Yet, they did, and they said: "I hope our cessation of the activities in the area of cluster munitions would enable our removal from prohibited investment firms and allow investors to consider Lockheed Martin for inclusion in their portfolios."[1]

This suggests that pressure from the financial world had had an impact. In Stop Explosive Investments' conversations with financial institutions there was clear feedback that the campaign and pressure from investors had contributed to Lockheed Martin's decision to end its (future) involvement in cluster-munitions-related activities.

Three other producers of cluster munitions have stated they are no longer involved in the production of (parts of) cluster munitions: Roketsan (Turkey), L-3 Communications (United States), and Singapore Technologies Engineering (Singapore). Singapore Technologies Engineering's change in policy can be attributed to the pressure of the Stop Explosive Investments campaign.

That shows how these reports, and the campaigns associated with them, can and do make a difference. It has worked with nuclear weapons too—as a divestment and boycott campaign drove General Electric to end its involvement with nuclear weapons in 1993 by altering the cost–benefit ratio for GE to be in the nuclear weapons business.

How do you start?

Step 1: Find out if your bank is an investor in nuclear-weapons producers. Use the report at www.dontbankonthebomb.com. The website is conveniently organized by country or alphabetically—you can pick whichever is easiest for you.

Step 2: Contact the bank (or pension fund, or asset management agent, etc.). TRY TO CLIMB AS HIGH AS YOU CAN. Campaigning efforts are more effective if you are able to get in contact with members of the board of directors. If the board of directors gets involved in your topic, you are halfway there. Most of the time, it will be difficult to contact someone on the board of directors, so it is important to find people who are involved in the decision-making process on policies relating to investments. The people you contact should be in a position to influence internal company policies.

Now, they may come back and say things like "nuclear weapons are not illegal." Neither is pornography, but that doesn't mean I want my pension fund financing it!

Step 3: Go public! Even the threat of going public with a campaign against a bank can be enough to push it to change policies. We've seen this with the German Commerzbank, where managers were mortified that they were a target for investing in nuclear-weapons producers. They issued statements in response to planned demonstrations giving a time-bound framework for highest-level policy changes.

ABP, a Dutch pension fund, has also been forced to change where it invests, and it didn't take a whole lot of campaigning to make that happen—but a Dutch TV program covered the *Don't Bank on the Bomb* report, and the ABP representative promised in 2013 they'd change the policy. They didn't, and so the TV program ran a survey of ABP's clients to demonstrate that they didn't want to have their retirement funded by nuclear-weapons-related investments.

Stigmatization works, and these efforts are demonstrating a whole-of-society opposition to unacceptable weapons. Just as divestment campaigns were part of the broader efforts to end apartheid in South Africa, this campaign is one piece of the global effort to stigmatize, outlaw, and eliminate nuclear weapons.

Divestment is not the only step that needs to be taken on the path to a world without nuclear weapons, but it is an important one. A coordinated global effort for divestment from nuclear-weapons producers can help put a halt to modernization programs, strengthen the international norm against nuclear weapons, and support negotiations on a nuclear-weapons ban.

In examining concrete, effective legal measures, legal provisions, and norms that will need to be concluded to attain and maintain a world without nuclear weapons, we cannot overlook the relationship between the financial and nuclear-weapons production industries.

Some financial institutions, including government funds, have already opted to exclude nuclear-weapons companies from their investment portfolios. It is time for others to end their voluntary involvement in the companies that are involved in the production and maintenance of the global weapons of mass destruction arsenal.

Sample Letter:

Dear Chief Executive Officer,

I am writing to you as a concerned customer of your bank. I recently read a report indicating that your bank is financing companies involved in the production of nuclear weapons.

Any use of nuclear weapons would violate fundamental rules of international law and have catastrophic humanitarian and environmental consequences. I strongly encourage you to divest from these companies without delay.

Other banks have instituted policies prohibiting these types of investments, demonstrating support for worldwide efforts to abolish nuclear weapons. I hope that you will assist rather than impede efforts to eliminate this ultimate threat to our future.

I want my savings to help secure my future and that of my family, not undermine it. Unless you can reassure me that you will no longer invest in nuclear-weapons producers, I intend to move my funds elsewhere.

I look forward to your response to these concerns.

Yours sincerely,

C.C.

CONCERNED CUSTOMER

19

The Heroic Marshall Islanders: Nuclear Zero Lawsuits

David Krieger

Between 1946 and 1958 the United States conducted sixty-seven nuclear tests in the Marshall Islands. The tests had the equivalent power of 1.6 Hiroshima bombs being exploded daily for twelve years. Some of the islands and atolls in the Marshall Islands became too radioactive to inhabit. The people of the Republic of the Marshall Islands were treated as guinea pigs for the United States to study, and they continue to suffer. They have never received fair or adequate compensation for their injuries resulting from the U.S. nuclear testing program.

On March 1, 1954, the United States conducted a nuclear test on the island of Bikini in the Marshall Islands. The bomb, detonated in a test known as Castle Bravo, had a thousand times the explosive power of the Hiroshima bomb. It contaminated the Bikini atoll and several other islands in the Marshall Islands, including Rongelap (one hundred miles away) and Utirik (three hundred miles away), as well as fishing vessels more than a hundred miles from the detonation. Crew members aboard the Japanese vessel *Lucky Dragon* were severely irradiated and one crew member died as a result of radiation poisoning. March 1 is known internationally as "Nuclear Free and Independent Pacific Day" or "Bikini Day." Marshall Islands former foreign minister Tony de Brum remembers the Bravo explosion as "a jolt on my soul that never left me."[1]

The Victims as Heroes

On April 24, 2014, after more than a year and a half of planning and preparations, the Marshall Islands filed lawsuits against nine nuclear-armed states in the International Court of Justice in The Hague and against the United States separately in U.S. Federal District Court in San Francisco. The Marshall Islanders sought no compensation in these lawsuits, but rather declaratory and injunctive relief declaring the nuclear-armed states to be in breach of their nuclear disarmament obligations and ordering them to fulfill these obligations by commencing within one year to negotiate in good faith for an end to the nuclear arms race and for nuclear disarmament.[2]

The lawsuits refered to obligations under the nuclear Non-Proliferation Treaty and under customary international law. Regarding the latter, they relied upon a portion of the Court's 1996 Advisory Opinion on the illegality of the threat or use of nuclear weapons, in which the Court stated: "There exists an obligation to pursue in good faith and bring to a conclusion negotiations leading to nuclear disarmament in all its aspects under strict and effective international control."[3]

The Marshall Islands is the mouse that roared; it is David standing against the nine nuclear goliaths; it is the friend not willing to let friends drive drunk on nuclear power. Most of all, the Marshall Islands stood for all humanity against those countries that are perpetuating the risk of nuclear war and the nuclear extinction of humanity and other forms of complex life on the planet. The courage and foresight of the Marshall Islanders are a harbinger of hope that should give hope to us all.

The Current Status of the Nuclear Zero Lawsuits

In the American case, the U.S. government filed a motion to dismiss the lawsuit against it on jurisdictional grounds, including those of standing and political question doctrine. On February 3, 2015, the federal judge, a George W. Bush appointee, granted the U.S. government's motion. The Marshall Islands has filed an appeal of the lower court's decision to the Ninth Circuit Court of Appeals, and are awaiting the Appeal Court's ruling.

At the International Court of Justice, cases against the three countries that accept the compulsory jurisdiction of the court—India, Pakistan, and the United Kingdom—are in process. In the case against the U.S., the Court voted 8 to 8 with the Court president's vote deciding that there was insufficient evidence of a dispute between the parties. On the same grounds, the Court voted 8 to 7 to dismiss the case against India and Pakistan.

Of the other six nuclear-armed countries that do not accept the compulsory jurisdiction of the International Court of Justice none has accepted the Marshall Islands' invitation to engage in the lawsuits. Only China has explicitly said that it will not do so.

An important observation about the lawsuits is that there was been reticence by the nuclear-armed states to have the issue of their obligations for nuclear disarmament heard by the courts. It would appear that the nuclear-armed countries are not eager to have their citizens or the people of the world know about their legal obligations to negotiate in good faith for nuclear disarmament or about their breaches of those obligations. Nor do they want the courts to order them to fulfill those obligations.

The Lawsuits Are About More than the Law

With regard to the legal aspects of these lawsuits, they were about whether treaties matter. They were about whether the most powerful nations are to be bound by the same rules as the rest of the international community. They were about whether a treaty can stand up with only half of the bargain fulfilled. They were about who gets to decide if treaty obligations are being met. Do all parties to a treaty stand on equal footing, or do the powerful have special rules specifically for them? They were also about the strength of customary international law to bind nations to civilized behavior.

These lawsuits were about more than just the law. They were also about leadership, boldness, courage, justice, wisdom, and, ultimately, about survival.

Leadership. If the most powerful countries won't lead, then other countries must. The Marshall Islands, a small island country, has demonstrated this leadership, both on ending climate chaos and on eliminating the nuclear weapons threat to humanity.

Boldness. Many in civil society have been calling for boldness in relation to the failure of the nuclear-armed countries to fulfill their obligations to negotiate in good faith to end the nuclear arms race and to achieve complete nuclear disarmament. The status quo has been littered with broken promises that have become hard to tolerate. Instead of negotiating in good faith for an end to the nuclear arms race "at an early date," the nuclear-armed countries have engaged in massive programs of modernization of their nuclear arsenals (nuclear weapons, delivery systems, and infrastructure). Such modernization of the U.S. nuclear arsenal alone is anticipated to cost a trillion dollars over the next three decades. Nuclear modernization by all nuclear-armed countries will ensure that nuclear weapons are deployed throughout the twenty-first century and beyond. The Marshall Islands boldly challenged the status quo with the Nuclear Zero lawsuits.

Courage. The Marshall Islands stands for all humanity in bringing these lawsuits. They could be viewed as David standing against the nine nuclear-armed Goliaths. But the Marshall Islands is a David acting nonviolently, using the courts and the law instead of a slingshot. The Marshall Islands has shown us by its actions what courage looks like.

Justice. The law should always be about justice. In the case of nuclear weapons, both the law and justice call for a level playing field, one in which no country has possession of nuclear weapons. That is the bargain of the Nuclear Non-Proliferation Treaty and the requirement of customary international law. The Marshall Islands took legal action seeking justice in the international community.

Wisdom. The lawsuits were about the wisdom to confront the hubris of the nuclear-armed countries. The arrogance of power is dangerous, and the arrogance of reliance upon nuclear weapons could be fatal for all humanity.

Survival. At their core, the Nuclear Zero lawsuits were about survival. They were about making nuclear war, by design or accident or miscalculation, impossible because there would no longer be nuclear weapons to threaten humanity. Without nuclear weapons in the world, there can be no nuclear war, no nuclear famine, no nuclear terrorism, no overriding threat to the human species and the future of humanity.

The dream of ending the nuclear-weapons threat to humanity cannot be the dream of just the Marshall Islanders; it must become our collective dream as well—and not only for today, but for the human future. We must challenge the "experts" and officials who tell us, "Don't worry, be happy" with the nuclear status quo.

The people of the world should follow the lead of the Marshall Islanders. If they can lead, we can support them. If they can be bold and courageous, we can join them. If they can demand that international law be based on justice, we can stand with them. If they can act wisely and confront hubris, with all its false assumptions, we can do the same. If they can take seriously the threat to human survival inherent in our most dangerous weapons, so can we. The Marshall Islands is showing us the way forward, breaking cocoons of complacency and demonstrating a conversion of hearts.

I am proud to be associated with the Marshall Islands and its extraordinary former foreign minister, Tony de Brum. As a consultant to the Marshall Islands, the Nuclear Age Peace Foundation has worked to build the legal teams that supported the Nuclear Zero lawsuits. We built a consortium of more than one hundred civil society organizations that supported the lawsuits. We also created a way for individuals to add their voices of support with a brief petition. Over 5 million people signed the petition supporting the Nuclear Zero lawsuits. You can find out more at the campaign website, www.nuclearzero.org.

20

Persistent Violence and Silent Suffering: Marshallese Migrants in Washington State

Holly Barker

The pain, horrors, and suffering of the Cold War are not over. This was not a war that was never fought; it was a war that amassed U.S. nuclear strength and created thousands of Cold War veterans, including U.S. servicemen, Native Americans who had their lands mined and pillaged for uranium, and, of course, the people of the Marshall Islands, who experienced the equivalent of 1.6 Hiroshima-sized bombs every day for the twelve-year period between 1946 and 1958.

Thinking of the Cold War as a distant relic is a privilege as it underscores the comfort and distance from hardship enjoyed by decision makers in Washington, D.C., and the nuclear-weapons laboratories. These laboratories earned large contracts during the Cold War that deepened the nexus between U.S. economic and military interests, and provided justification to threaten our foes with nuclear retaliation. But this distance from the lives of the Marshall Islanders also includes the U.S. public that remains ignorant of U.S. activities during this time period—not because Americans are cold or uncaring, but because this top-secret military history was not known or discussed. This ignorance makes Americans victims of the Cold War as well, albeit in a much different form.

For most Americans, the Cold War is over. But what happened to the Marshallese people in the intervening years? What happened to the radiation? What happened to their lands? What is the quality of life like for the people who lived but saw their land, health, culture, and economy decimated by Cold War terror? It is important to follow the people of the Marshall Islands on their continued exodus from the homelands they can no longer inhabit because of residual radiation levels to distant locations in search of health care and economic opportunities. In particular, we must consider the structural violence that is a persistent reality for Marshallese migrants to Washington State and other locations. Structural violence is a term made popular by anthropologist and physician Paul Farmer as he considered the ways that our institutions, through policy and practice, render violence on marginalized people by failing to provide adequate support so they can live a healthy life.[1] The structural violence that fails to provide adequate health care to Marshallese on their home islands migrates along with the Marshallese to the United States, where they remain on the outside looking in, and unable to access the state-of-the-art services that their posttrusteeship bodies need.

Structural Violence: The Failure to Provide Life-Saving Health Care in the Marshall Islands

In terms of radioactive iodine alone, the United States released 6.3 billion curies of iodine-131 into the atmosphere as a result of its testing in the Marshall Islands—an amount 42 times greater than the 150 million curies released by the atmospheric testing in Nevada, 150 times greater than the estimated 40 million curies released as a result of the Chernobyl nuclear accident, and 8,500 times greater than the 739,000 curies released from Atomic Energy Commission operations at Hanford, Washington.

After the deployment of atomic weapons during World War II, the United States needed to learn more about the capabilities of its newest weapon—more information than the destruction of Hiroshima and Nagasaki provided. The United States decided to make a proving ground out of its small islands in the northern Pacific

Ocean that the United States acquired as part of a United Nations trust territory following the war. As the trust territory administrator, the United States promised to safeguard the well-being of its inhabitants. Many people assume that the islands were deserted during the Cold War tests, but they weren't. In 1958, the final year of the testing program, the census counted over fourteen thousand people living in the Marshall Islands.[2]

On the atolls of Bikini and Enewetak in the Marshall Islands, the United States detonated sixty-seven atmospheric atomic and thermonuclear weapons from 1946 to 1958. From nuclear weapons tests in the Marshall Islands, the United States learned how its naval fleet would survive a nuclear attack. In 1946, U.S. researchers anchored navy vessels, including the Japanese flagship captured at the end of World War II, the *Nagato*, in Bikini's lagoon. While most of the weapons tests took place above ground to study the impacts of the blast and fallout on the land and people, detonations such as Test Baker took place underwater to research the impacts of the United States's newest weapon when unleashed directly into the ocean. Test Baker debilitated and sunk many vessels that remain on the bottom of Bikini's lagoon today. The world knows this location as the bikini bathing suit, or the home of SpongeBob SquarePants, but not as the sacred homelands of the people of Pikinni, known as Bikini.[3]

Also in the Marshall Islands, the United States detonated its largest weapon ever tested, the Bravo shot of March 1, 1954, the equivalent of one thousand Hiroshima-sized bombs. Bravo exposed the crew of a Japanese fishing boat near Bikini, Marshallese residents downwind from Bikini, and U.S. servicemen to levels of radiation that caused death and lifelong illness. Following Bravo, U.S. government researchers evacuated some of the islanders and enrolled them in a secret medical experiment, called Project 4.1, to study the effects of radiation on human beings. Later, the U.S. government resettled the unwitting participants in this program on an island highly contaminated with radiation to learn firsthand how human beings ingest and absorb radiation from their environment.

During the Cold War, the United States made immeasurable political strides as nuclear superiority guaranteed status as a superpower and ushered in a period of nuclear deterrence. This political advancement of the United States came with a high price for the Marshallese, however, whose health and environment continue to display the scars of U.S. nuclear achievements.

Recently the U.S. National Cancer Institute predicted that the Marshallese will experience hundreds more future cancer cases directly linked to the U.S. nuclear-weapons testing program. The radiological illnesses from the testing program continue to overwhelm the capabilities of the public health infrastructure in the Marshall Islands.

Despite the radiation levels released in the Marshall Islands, the indisputable link between cancer and radiation exposure, and the recent NCI predictions, there is no oncologist in the Marshall Islands, no chemotherapy, no cancer registry, and no nationwide screening program for early detection of cancer. Thus, the United States released large amounts of radiation in the Marshall Islands, radiation exposure causes cancer, and there is no cancer care available in the Marshall Islands. This is abhorrent, considering that the United States was the only governing authority of the Marshall Islands when it used the islands to test its weapons. The only way to treat cancer and have an opportunity to survive is to leave the country. This is a poignant example of structural violence, as the fact that the U.S. government fails to provide cancer care means that Marshallese die from cancers that could be treatable elsewhere.

Structural Violence: The Inability to Access Health Care for Low-Income, Legal Migrants in the United States

Currently, Marshallese are able to migrate to the United States to live, work, and go to school. They do not require a visa because of the unique history between the United States and the Marshall

Islands, a bond that enabled the United States to exert its right to detonate weapons of mass destruction in the islands.

Given that the nuclear weapons testing by the United States shaped all aspects of life, and the destruction of life, beginning with the Cold War, it seems reasonable to Marshallese citizens who migrate to the United States that Americans should know about the U.S. government's activities in the islands. It seems reasonable to expect compassion, empathy, and care. Sadly, this is not the case, and our failure to know about this history and its consequences denies us the opportunity to advocate for and support the Marshallese people who enter our communities.

The Marshallese come to the United States seeking access to opportunities not available in the Marshall Islands as a result of U.S. decision making during and after the trusteeship. In Washington State, Marshallese arrive willing to both engage with and contribute to their communities, but also with needs: needs for health care, education, and employment opportunities. Marshallese contribute to communities through church, school, and service projects, like the Marshallese in Lynnwood, Washington, who organize to feed the homeless twice each month. They pay taxes, contribute to Social Security, and serve in every branch of the U.S. armed services to protect the interests of the United States.

As with other migrant communities that lack the health and educational resources to reach their full capabilities, many Marshallese struggle with poverty. In Washington State, Marshallese adults are less likely to have a bachelor's degree than those from any other ethnic group.[4]

For low-income, legal residents in the United States, the federal government provides Medicaid benefits to serve as a safety net to extend health care benefits to those who are least able to access it. The people of the Marshall Islands—people who are in the United States legally, people whose homelands are irradiated, people whose bodies carry the radiogenic burdens of the Cold War—are not eligible for Medicaid.

The failure to extend Medicaid to the Marshallese is another form of structural violence. Our policies that exclude Marshallese from access to health care designed for low-income, legal residents means that migrants continue to be excluded from U.S. health care services. What does this mean for the Marshallese? For Lucky Juda, who was in utero during the Bikini people's evacuation of their home islands for the Bravo detonation in 1954, it means that he was denied access to health care. Lucky and his family were part of the group of Bikinians who were prematurely resettled by the U.S. government on Bikini in the 1970s when the United States declared that Bikini was "safe" for human habitation. After determining that the Bikinians absorbed more cesium than any known population as a result of their relocation, Lucky and the other Bikinians left Bikini, and Bikini remains uninhabited to this day. Bikini is Lucky's homeland, the land which he inherits from his ancestors, yet he cannot access it, and cannot utilize the resources available to him for food (coconuts, breadfruit) or for economics (fish, copra).

In 2016, Lucky developed a heart condition that could not be treated in the Marshall Islands. He came to Washington State to visit his daughter and to access health care. Lucky was shocked by what he encountered in Washington.

Lucky, whose name signals the hopes of his parents that he would meet a better fate, has not been fortunate. He represents the continued violence of Cold War nuclear testing. Lucky cannot access his homelands because of radiation contamination. He lives in a nation with Third World health care yet has health care challenges created by First World arrogance. Thinking that the United States, which shaped every aspect of his life, has a responsibility to support his health care needs, Lucky came to Washington.

In Washington, Lucky encountered health care workers who had never heard of the Marshall Islands, or had any understanding or knowledge of the ways the United States destroyed many aspects of Lucky's health and livelihood. Lucky felt disrespected, and he felt sad. He could not access Medicaid in the United States. He decided that there was no reason to stay in Washington, a place where people do not acknowledge or understand his hardships and a place where he could not access health care for low-income patients, like him. Without receiving adequate attention from health care providers in Washington, Lucky decided to return to the Marshall Islands. In the Honolulu Airport, Lucky had a heart attack and had to be rushed to the hospital for emergency surgery. He was not fit to fly or to travel from Washington, yet it was pointless to stay in a location where providers would not care for him. What options does Lucky have? He is returning to the Marshall Islands where there is inadequate health care. The United States has failed Lucky at every turn: in the Marshall Islands, where he cannot access the health care he needs, and in the United States, where he cannot access the health care that is not available to him.

The Violence of Ignorance

The people of the Marshall Islands deserve our appreciation for the monumental sacrifices they incurred during the Cold War. More than a decade ago, the Marshall Islands submitted a petition to the U.S. Congress for additional assistance, primarily to create the capacity to respond to the health care burdens resulting from the U.S. nuclear weapons testing program. The U.S. government has not responded to the Marshall Island government's request for assistance.

On March 1 of every year, on the anniversary of the Bravo detonation that changed the course of their lives, Marshallese in the United States huddle together, pray, cry, remember loved ones, and long for their homelands. They hope and ask for the United States to help provide them with the health care they need. They pray that the violence and hurt will be muted. In Salem, Oregon, in Fayetteville, Arkansas, in Enid, Oklahoma, these prayers go unanswered and beg all of us to consider how we allow this violence to continue, how we allow ourselves to stay in our privileged bubbles shielded from the horrors of the Cold War that reside with our neighbors. On March 1, 2016, during a day of remembrance held at the Burke Museum in Seattle, Lucky Juda reflected:

> The whole Marshall Islands is condemned from the bomb. There is a lot of people that got sick. . . . Thyroid and cancer and a lot more . . . Tumors. All kinds of sickness. It is very sad for all of us people of the Marshall Islands. . . . The Americans thought that we are just like the animals. We are guinea pigs. . . . These are some of the things that I think about everyday. When I am thinking that all things that are going on, I wonder why did God let me live. Why was I born when all of this is going on. I shouldn't have been born, I should have died at that time.[5]

The atrocities of the nuclear era are not something that happened just to people on far-flung islands of the Pacific; they are something that happened to all of us. While the Marshallese suffer the health care and other burdens of the era, we suffer, too; we suffer from ignorance—the ability to ignore. We suffer from the deafness of the needs of our neighbors. We are all victims of the Cold War.

21

Adding Democracy to Nuclear Policy

Kennette Benedict

The 2016 U.S. presidential campaign has, among other things, reminded the public that the president has the sole authority to launch a nuclear attack. While public discussion focused on the temperament, judgment, and character of the person occupying the office of the presidency, it has also raised the larger question about the democratic legitimacy of a single person being able to launch a nuclear war. As William Broad and David Sanger of the *New York Times* put it, "Is there any check on a president's power to launch nuclear arms that could destroy entire cities or nations?" Their answer is no, not really.[1]

As President Richard Nixon observed in 1974, "I can go back into my office and pick up the telephone and in 25 minutes 70 million people will be dead."[2]

As it stands today, long after the fall of the Soviet Union and the perceived need to act quickly in response to its actions, Americans have continued to cede the right to decide when the nation will launch a nuclear war to a single person. We have no voice in the most significant decision the U.S. government can make—whether to destroy another society with weapons of mass destruction.

To safeguard our democracy and reduce the risk of a nuclear weapons launch, the new administration should: place our nuclear weapons on a much lower level of launch readiness, release to the public more information about the nuclear weapons in our own arsenals, include legislators and outside experts in its nuclear posture review, and recognize Congress's authority to declare war as a prerequisite to any use of nuclear weapons.

Of all the powers of the U.S. president, that of commander in chief of nuclear military forces is the most grave, and carries with it the responsibility for the welfare of the world. The current posture and readiness of U.S. nuclear forces gives the president power to wipe out entire nations within thirty minutes of a launch command.

Normally, under the Constitution, only Congress has the power to declare war. Yet, our nuclear doctrine of deterrence and prompt retaliation in the face of incoming missiles requires rapid reaction with no time for consultation with Congress or even with cabinet members and national security advisors. The result is that the most consequential decision a president can make, with the potential to obliterate nations and kill millions of people, is made in secret and without deliberation.

How is it that, in the longest surviving democracy, the power to wreak the most catastrophic destruction in the history of the world is held by a single person? Such power completely contradicts the constitutional checks and balances that the Founders created in 1787. It is long past time to reexamine policies that place such massively destructive power in the hands of one person.

Current nuclear doctrine is a carryover from the Cold War between the United States and the Soviet Union. The nuclear age dawned at the end of World War II, when President Harry Truman ordered the atomic bombings of Hiroshima and Nagasaki.

But that decision was made by a commander in chief in a time of war. Immediately following World War II, the militarization of conflict with the Soviet Union led U.S. presidents and national security policy advisors to use the new nuclear arsenal as a means of *deterring* the Soviets.

In particular, two assumptions of nuclear deterrence fly in the face of democratic norms—speed and secrecy. The need for speed derives from the nuclear postures of the two superpowers. Not only did each build large arsenals of weapons to overwhelm the adversary, but they also maintained the arsenals in a high state of launch readiness. In the event of a surprise attack, each could launch missiles even before the enemy's had exploded on their soil, using their nuclear capability rather than seeing it destroyed by enemy incoming missiles. The idea was to "use them or lose them" in the face of Soviet attack. Since it takes only thirty minutes for an intercontinental ballistic missile to reach the enemy, neither side had time for deliberation. And certainly there was no time for Congress to declare war. However, in a supreme irony of history, by placing speedy retaliation against an authoritarian regime in the hands of the president, a democratically elected president became an authoritarian leader.

Throughout the Cold War, the United States and the Soviet Union maintained secrecy about their own capabilities to keep the other side off balance and to gain technical superiority. In the 1940s, the United States sought to keep bomb designs secret with the unrealistic hope that the Soviets would never figure out how to make an atomic bomb. That hope was dashed in 1949 when the Soviets tested their first atomic bomb, and again in 1953 when they tested their first thermonuclear bomb just a few months after the United States tested theirs. Although the need for secrecy was invoked to keep information about the bomb from other countries, knowledge leaked and weapons have proliferated ever since 1945. Yet, government leaders have also invoked the need for secrecy to keep information about nuclear war fighting from their own citizens. Ironically, officials in the Soviet Union knew more about U.S. nuclear forces and capabilities than U.S. citizens did.

In the early 1990s, with the demise of the Soviet bloc and normalization of relations between Russia and the United States, it would have made sense to rethink nuclear deterrence and especially the need for quick launch and retaliation. Beginning in 1994, the superpowers were working together to dismantle their nuclear weapons through a cooperative program that provided transparency about nuclear forces and even partial sharing of war plans. Yet, neither military command revisited the fundamentals of nuclear deterrence—a doctrine devised during the most hostile days of the Cold War. Nor was there an opening up of the policy-making process to include legislative members or interested citizens in either country.

Today, continued secrecy and assumed requirements of high launch readiness prevent democratic consideration of how weapons should be deployed or even serious public discussion of how much money to spend on them. The result is a set of policies that, in effect, could perpetrate mass murder of innocent civilians in other countries without the explicit consent of the citizens in this democracy.

When it comes to nuclear weapons, then, the conduct of war lies wholly outside the social contract between citizens and their government. With the capability to launch nuclear weapons without a declaration of war by Congress, the president becomes a tyrant, acting on his or her own outside the democratic institutions provided for in the Constitution.

Even though they had no way of envisioning the advent of the nuclear age, the Framers of the U.S. Constitution understood the dangers of tyranny and lodged the power to declare war and provide resources for war making with Congress rather than the president. They believed that ceding such power to the executive would contribute to lawlessness among nations and a state of perpetual war. The Founders viewed citizen participation in decisions about war as a necessary check on the power of the president and as a way to prevent the tyranny they had fought against as colonists under British rule.[3]

Some see an antidote to this nuclear tyranny in today's popular election of the president, who is said to represent us all. Yet, we are a nation of laws and institutions for a reason. Individuals can fall ill, be corrupted, or exercise poor judgment. That's why the U.S. Constitution places checks and balances on the actions of individual leaders by providing for three bodies of government—the executive, the legislative, and the judiciary. When it comes to waging war, the Constitution makes a special provision: the largest deliberative body in our government is given the responsibility to decide. Placing our own citizens in harm's way to kill and injure those in other societies is the most consequential decision a nation can make. The Founders understood that such a grave responsibility should be lodged in the institution that is the most broadly representative of the population and that affords the greatest opportunity for deliberation.

What is the remedy for this nuclear tyranny? Measures should be taken immediately that would place the United States on a path to more democratic decision making when it comes to the use of nuclear weapons. First, nuclear weapons should be placed on a much lower level of launch readiness, even to the point of removing warheads from missiles until the time when they may be needed. The United States and Russia are the only two countries that have nuclear bombs ready to go within minutes of a command; yet, we are no longer locked in a struggle for world domination, and the risks of accidental or unauthorized launch are too great to continue this unnecessary policy. Such a reduction in launch readiness would immediately reduce the risk of launch by a president without consultation.

Second, the U.S. government can publish information about the nuclear weapons we have in our arsenals, setting an example for other countries to follow, and, most important, provide information to its own citizens to use in their discussions about nuclear war. In fact, the Defense Department in May 2016 and the State Department in April 2015 already have begun to declare the numbers of active weapons in U.S. arsenals, as well as those awaiting dismantlement. Information about the plans for those arsenals, including potential targets and estimates of their effects, would help inform voters about what is at stake when we talk about nuclear war. Ideally, the information would inspire legislators to hold public hearings about the military use of these world-altering weapons, along with the costs of their deployment and maintenance.

Third, the next U.S. nuclear posture review should include consultations with legislators and interested constituencies. As the administration prepares for nuclear war, the nation is entitled to participate in this most consequential planning. The nuclear posture review is, in effect, our rationale for when and why it is acceptable to use nuclear weapons. As such, it should be subjected to special scrutiny, as it is being reviewed and changed by the new administration.

Fourth, Article I, section 8 of the U.S. Constitution, which gives Congress the power to declare war, should be reinstated as the law of the land. Despite near-constant U.S. military action around the world since 1945, Congress has not formally declared a war since World War II. Neither has it taken the lead in deciding when and whether to use nuclear weapons. In this context, the initiative of Sen. Edward Markey (D-MA) and Rep. Ted Lieu (D-CA) is especially welcome. Their proposed legislation, the Restricting First Use of Nuclear Weapons Act of 2017, would prohibit the president from launching nuclear weapons without a declaration of war from Congress, except in response to a nuclear attack. A president may choose to ignore such a new law, and even invoke the War Powers Act of 1973 to use nuclear weapons; but to do so would further deepen the public's alienation from their government and contribute to the decline of public trust in our democratic institutions.

Without congressional deliberation and citizen participation in the gravest decisions of life and death, our democracy is greatly diminished. Citizens are treated as children who don't deserve a voice in how our country's nuclear weapons are deployed. Experts claim they are the only ones who have sufficient training and knowledge to make policy choices about the fate of our society. That is not how a democracy should work.

It is time for citizens to exercise their democratic rights and demand a major role in nuclear weapons policy making. The new administration should respond with plans to reduce secrecy and increase wider participation in how our nuclear weapons are used.

The likely outcome, once the public fully understands the consequences of nuclear war, is a greatly reduced role for nuclear weapons in national security policy. The certain outcome is a restoration of our democratic institutions.

Notes

Introduction—Helen Caldicott

1. Jane Mayer, "Donald Trump's Ghostwriter Tells All," *New Yorker*, July 25, 2016; James Wilkinson, "'Please God don't give this man the nuclear codes': 'Ghostwriter' of Donald Trump's 'The Art of the Deal' warns that Trump could cause atomic Armageddon—but says The Donald 'has given up' on winning election," *Daily Mail*, October 16, 2016.

2. Helen Caldicott, *The New Nuclear Danger: George W. Bush's Military-Industrial Complex* (New York: The New Press, 2004).

3. Bruce Blair, "Could U.S.-Russian Tensions Go Nuclear?" *Politico*, November 27, 2015.

4. Ibid.

5. Ibid.

6. Ibid.

7. Ibid.

8. Ibid.

9. John Pilger, "The Coming War on China," *New Internationalist*, April 21, 2017.

10. Bruce Blair, "Could U.S.-Russian Tensions Go Nuclear?"

11. Ibid.

12. *The New Nuclear Danger*, 16.

13. Posts by Andrew Emett, Global Research, March 20, 2016; The Free Thought Project, March 19, 2016, www.thefreethoughtproject.com /14-airmen-responsible-guarding-u.s.nukes-caught-cocaine.

1. Assessing Global Catastrophic Risk—Seth D. Baum

[There are no notes for this chapter. —ed.]

2. Modernization of Nuclear Weaponry—Hans Kristensen

1. Hans M. Kristensen and Robert S. Norris, "Nuclear Notebook," *Bulletin of the Atomic Scientists*, 2017, http://explore.tandfonline.com/page/pgas/rbul-nuclear-notebooks/.

3. Nuclear Smoke and the Climatic Effects of Nuclear War—Alan Robock

1. A. Robock, L. Oman, G.L. Stenchikov, O.B. Toon, C. Bardeen, and R.P. Turco, "Climatic consequences of regional nuclear conflicts," *Atm. Chem. Phys.* 7 (2007), 2003–2012.

2. Figure 2 from A. Robock, L. Oman, and G.L. Stenchikov, "Nuclear winter revisited with a modern climate model and current nuclear arsenals: Still catastrophic consequences," *J. Geophys. Res.* 112 (2007), D13107, doi:2006JD008235, used with permission.

3. A. Stenke, et al., "Climate and chemistry effects of a regional scale nuclear conflict," *Atmos. Chem. Phys.* 13 (2013), 9713-9729, doi:10.5194/acp-13-9713-2013; M.J. Mills, O.B. Toon, J. Lee-Taylor, and A. Robock, "Multi-decadal global cooling and unprecedented ozone loss following a regional nuclear conflict." Earth's Future 2 (2014), 161-176, doi:10.1002/2013EF000205.

4. L. Xia, A. Robock, M. Mills, A. Stenke, and I. Helfand, "Decadal reduction of Chinese agriculture after a regional nuclear war," *Earth's Future*, 3 (2015), 37-48, doi:10.1002/2014EF000283.

5. M. Özdoğan, A. Robock, and C. Kucharik, "Impacts of a nuclear war in South Asia on soybean and maize production in the Midwest United States," *Climatic Change*, 116 (2013), 373-387, doi:10.1007/s10584-012-051 8-1.

6. A. Robock, L. Oman, and G.L. Stenchikov, "Nuclear winter revisited with a modern climate model and current nuclear arsenals: Still catastrophic consequences," *J. Geophys. Res.* 112 (2007), D13107, doi:2006JD008235.

7. M. Hertsgaard, "Mikhail Gorbachev explains what's rotten in Russia," *Salon*, September 7, 2000.

8. Carl Sagan, "Nuclear war and climatic catastrophe: Some policy implications," *Foreign Affairs*, Winter 1983/84, No. 62202, 257–292.

9. Dr. Seuss, *The Lorax* (New York: Random House, 1971).

4. Addicted to Weapons—Bruce Gagnon

1. Peter Korzun, "NATO pushing for Military Buildup in the Black Sea," online journal of the Strategic Culture Foundation, January 11, 2016, www.strategic-culture.org/news/2016/11/01/nato-pushing-for-military -buildup-in-black-sea.html.

2. Thomas Friedman, "Parallel Parking in the Arctic Circle," *New York Times*, March 29, 2014.

3. Li Bin, "China and the New U.S. Missile Defense in East Asia" Carnegie Endowment for International Peace, September 6, 2012, http:// carnegieendowment.org/2012/09/06/china-and-new-u.s.-missile-defense -in-east-asia-pub-49297.

4. Zachary Keck, "Japan's building 2 Aegis Destroyers," *The Diplomat*, July 23, 2014.

5. Mark Weiner, "Pentagon delays decision on East Coast missile defense site touted for Fort Drum," *Syracuse.com*, December 5, 2016.

6. Nicholas Fandos, "U.S. Foreign Arms Deals Increased Nearly $10 Billion in 2014," *New York Times*, December 25, 2015.

7. Gary Chapman, "Military Spending and the American Economy," Context Institute, Winter 1989, www.context.org/iclib/ic20/chapman.

8. Nick Schwellenbach, "Study: Federal Spending on Defense Doesn't Create as Many Jobs as Education Spending," *Time*, September 21, 2011.

5. The Plutonium Problem—Bob Alvarez

1. en.wikipedia.org/wiki/Deuterium.

2. www.europarl.europa.eu/stoa/publications/studies/20001701_en .pdf.

3. Ibid.

4. Ibid.

5. www.sciencedirect.com/science?_ob=ArticleURL&_udi=B6WDV -45F54VV-K&_user=10&_rdoc=1&_fmt=&_orig=search&_ sort=d&view=c&_acct=C000050221&_version=1&_urlVersion=0&_useri d=10&md5=8100df10ae8e8b58c1e0a8ede2be6e61.

6. www.pubmedcentral.nih.gov/articlerender.fcgi?artid=1662259; www.pubmedcentral.nih.gov/articlerender.fcgi?tool=pubmed&pubmed id=8326267; jech.bmj.com/cgi/content/abstract/55/7/469.

7. www.europarl.europa.eu/stoa/publications/studies/20001701_en .pdf.

8. www.princeton.edu/~globsec/publications/pdf/13 1-2 alverez 43 86.pdf.

9. www.gao.gov/new.items/d03593.pdf;www.whistleblower.org/doc/20 07/gnepFINAL.pdf.

10. Ibid.

11. Ibid.

12. www.fissilematerials.org/.

13. Ibid.

14. www.nap.edu/catalog.php?record_id=4912.

15. www.nap.edu/catalog.php?record_id=11998.

6. Nuclear Weapons and Artificial Intelligence—Max Tegmark

I wish to thank Helen Caldicott for inviting me to give the talk upon which this paper is based, Jesse Galef for help transcribing it, Meia Chita-Tegmark for helpful feedback, and Will Nelson for careful proofreading.

1. H.M. Kristensen and R.S. Norris, "Worldwide Deployments of Nuclear Weapons," *Bull. Atomic Scientists* (2014), bos.sagepub.com /content/early/2014/08/26/0096340214547619.full.pdf.

2. www.justice.gov/civil/awards-date-04242015.

3. P.J. Crutzen and J.W. Birks, "The Atmosphere After a Nuclear War: Twilight at Noon," *Ambio* (1982), 11; R.P. Turco, O.B. Toon, T.P. Ackerman, J.B. Pollack, and C. Sagan, "Nuclear Winter: Global Consequences of Multiple Nuclear Explosions," *Science* 222 (1983), 1283–1292; V.V. Aleksandrov and G.L. Stenchikov, "On the Modeling of the Climatic Consequences of the Nuclear War," *Proc. Appl. Math* (1983), 21 pp., Comput. Cent., Russ. Acad. of Sci., Moscow; A. Robock, "Snow and Ice Feedbacks Prolong Effects of Nuclear Winter," *Nature* 310 (1984), 667–670.

4. G.A. Schmidt et al., "Present-Day Atmospheric Simulations Using GISS ModelE: Comparison to In Situ, Satellite, and Reanalysis Data," *J. Clim.* 19 (2006), 153–192; D. Koch, G.A. Schmidt, and C.V. Field, "Sulfur, Sea Salt, and Radionuclide Aerosols in GISS ModelE," *J. Geophys. Res.* 111 (2006), D06206.

5. A. Robock, L. Oman, and L. Stenchikov 2007, "Nuclear Winter Revisited with a Modern Climate Model and Current Nuclear Arsenals: Still Catastrophic Consequences," *J. Geophys. Res.* 12 (2007), D13107.

6. A. Robock and O.B. Toon, "Self-Assured Destruction: The Climate Impacts of Nuclear War," *Bulletin of Atomic Scientists*, September 1, 2012, www.thebulletin.org/2012/september/self-assured-destruction-climate -impacts-nuclear-war.

7. E. Schlosser, *Command and Control: Nuclear Weapons, the Damascus Accident, and the Illusion of Safety* (New York: Penguin, 2014).

8. L. Gronlund and D.C. Wright, "Depressed Trajectory SLBMs: A Technical Evaluation and Arms Control Possibilities," *Science & Global Security* 3 (1992), 101–159, www.princeton.edu/sgs/publications /sgs/pdf/3_1-2gronlund.pdf.

9. D. Kahneman, *Thinking, Fast and Slow*, (New York: Farrar, Straus and Giroux, 2013).

10. A. Robock, L. Oman, and L. Stenchikov, "Nuclear Winter Revisited with a Modern Climate Model and Current Nuclear Arsenals: Still Catastrophic Consequences," *J. Geophys. Res.* 12 (2007), D13107.

11. www.dontbankonthebomb.com.

12. www.futureoflife.org.

7. Weapons Scientists Up Close—Hugh Gusterson

1. Bruce Krasnow, "The Secret to Los Alamos' Wealth? Education," *Santa Fe New Mexican*, February 3, 2015, www.santafenewmexican .com/news/business/business-matters-the-secret-to-los-alamos-wealth -education/article_f99cf63b-7eb7-5cbb-9e21-a28d1cd7a2f3.html.

2. David Hoffman, *The Dead Hand: The Untold Story of the Cold War Arms Race and Its Dangerous Legacy* (New York: Doubleday, 2009); Eric Schlosser, *Command and Control: Nuclear Weapons, the Damascus Incident, and the Illusion of Safety* (New York: Penguin Books, 2013).

3. Harold Agnew, Interview. *Los Alamos Science Magazine* 2(2) (Summer/Fall 1981): 152–159.

4. Joseph Masco, "Nuclear Technoaesthetics: Sensory Politics from Trinity to the Virtual Bomb in Los Alamos," *American Ethnologist* 31(3) (2004), 349–73.

5. Elaine Woo, "Harold Agnew, Head of Atomic Laboratory, Dies at 92," *Washington Post*, October 2, 2013.

8. What Would Happen If an 800-Kiloton Nuclear Warhead Detonated Above Midtown Manhattan—Steven Starr, Lynn Eden, Theodore A. Postol

[There are no notes for this chapter. —ed.]

9. National Politics Versus National Security—Noam Chomsky

1. "It Is Two and a Half Minutes to Midnight: 2017 Doomsday Clock Statement," *Bulletin of the Atomic Scientists*, http://thebulletin.org/sites/ default/files/Final%202017%20Clock%20Statement.pdf.

2. www.umich.edu/~pugwash/Manifesto.html.

3. Larry Bartels, *Unequal Democracy* (Princeton, NJ: Princeton University Press, 2008); Martin Gilens, *Affluence and Influence* (Princeton, NJ: Princeton University Press, 2012).

4. Jo Confino, "How Concerned Are CEOs About Climate Change? Not at All," *The Guardian*, January 20, 2015.

5. See Benjamin Page, with Marshall Bouton, *The Foreign Policy Disconnect* (Chicago: University of Chicago Press, 2006); Noam Chomsky, *Failed States* (New York: Henry Holt & Co., 2006), chapter 4.

6. Jessica Mathews, *New York Review of Books* (March 19, 2015).

7. McGeorge Bundy, *Danger and Survival* (New York: Random House, 1988), 326.

8. Adam Ulam, "A Few Unresolved Mysteries About Stalin and the Cold War in Europe," *J. of Cold War Studies* 1.1 (Winter 1999); Melvyn Leffler, "Inside Enemy Archives," *Foreign Affairs* (July/August 1996).

9. Mary Elise Sarotte, *1989: the Struggle to Create Post–Cold War Europe* (Princeton, NJ: Princeton University Press, 2009); John Mearsheimer, "Why the Ukraine Crisis Is the West's Fault," *Foreign Affairs* (September/October 2014).

10. David M. Herszenhorn, "Ukraine Vote Takes Nation a Step Closer to NATO," *New York Times*, December 23, 2014.

11. Kenneth Waltz, "America as a Model for the World? A Foreign Policy Perspective," *PS: Political Science & Politics* (December 1991).

12. Noam Chomsky and Irene Gendzier, *Jerusalem Quarterly* 54 (Summer 2013).

13. Benjamin B. Fischer, "A Cold War Conundrum: The 1983 Soviet War Scare," summary, /library/center-for-the-study-of-intelligence/csi-publications/books-and-monographs/a-cold-war-conundrum/source.htm#Top of File.

14. Pavel Aksenov, "Stanislav Petrov: The Man Who May Have Saved the World," BBC Russian Service (September 26, 2013); Eric Schlosser, *Command and Control* (New York: Penguin, 2013), 447.

15. Seth Baum, "Nuclear War, the Black Swan We Can Never See," http://thebulletin.org/nuclear-war-black-swan-we-can-never-see7821.

16. Lee Butler, "Death by Deterrence," *Resurgence* 193 (March/April 1999).

17. Lee Butler, letter to M.P. Bill Graham, House of Commons, Canada, http://fas.org/news/canada/18-appa-e.htm.

10. Escalation Watch: Four Looming Flash Points Facing President Trump—Michael T. Klare

This article originally appeared on TomDispatch on January 17, 2017, www.tomdispatch.com/post/176231/tomgram%3A_michael_klare%2C_twenty-first-century_armageddons/#more.

1. Michael J. Mazaarr, "The Once and Future Order: What Comes After Hegemony?" *Foreign Affairs* (January 2017).

2. Teresa Welsh, "US Drops More Bombs in Obama's Final Year of Office Than in 2015," McClatchy DC, January 5, 2017, www.mcclatchydc.com/news/nation-world/national/article124842824.html; Jeffrey Goldberg, "The Obama Doctrine," *The Atlantic*, April 2016.

3. "Full Transcript: Second 2016 Presidential Debate," *Politico*, October 10, 2016.

4. Daniella Diaz and Jeremy Diamond, "Trump on Iran Ship Behavior: 'They Will Be Shot Out of the Water,'" CNN (September 9, 2016), www.cnn.com/2016/09/09/politics/donald-trump-iran/.

5. Tom Blackwell, "Mysterious and 'Arrogant' Vladimir Putin Seeks Russia's Return to Status of World Superpower," *National Post*, March 4, 2014, news.nationalpost.com/news/mysterious-and-arrogant-vladimir-putin-seeks-russias-return-to-status-of-world-superpower.

6. Chris Buckley, "Trump's and Xi's Differences Magnify Uncertainties Between U.S. and China," *New York Times*, December 19, 2016.

7. "The Threat from Russia," *The Economist*, October 22, 2016.

8. Eugene Rumer, "Russia and the Security of Europe," Carnegie Endowment for International Peace, June 30, 2016, www.carnegieendowment.org/2016/06/30/russia-and-security-of-europe-pub-63990.

9. "Iskander (SS-26 Stone) Short-Range Ballistic Missile," *Military Today*, www.military-today.com/missiles/iskander.htm; "New Russia Missiles in Kaliningrad Are Answer to U.S. Shield: Lawmaker," Reuters, November 21, 2016.

10. Tom Sauer, "Just Leave It: NATO's Nuclear Weapons Policy at the Warsaw Summit," Arms Control Association, June 2016, www.armscontrol.org/ACT/2016_06/Features/Just-Leave-It-NATOs-Nuclear-Weapons-Policy-at-the-Warsaw-Summit.

11. "Arms Control and Proliferation Profile: North Korea," Arms Control Association, November 2016, www.armscontrol.org/factsheets/northkoreaprofile.

12. Kelsey Davenport, "North Korea Conducts Fifth Nuclear Test," October 2016, www.armscontrol.org/ACT/2016_10/News/North-Korea-Conducts-Fifth-Nuclear-Test.

13. Jack Kim, "N. Korea Leader Tells Military to Be Ready to Use Nuclear Weapons," Reuters, March 7, 2016.

14. Tony Munroe and Jack Kim, "North Korea's Kim Says Close to Test Launch of ICBM," Reuters, January 1, 2017.

15. Mark Fitzpatrick, "North Korea: Obama's Prime Nonproliferation Failure," Arms Control Association, December 2016, www.armscontrol.org /ACT/2016_11/Features/North-Korea-Obamas-Prime-Nonproliferation -Failure; William J. Perry, "To Confront North Korea, Talk First and Get Tough Later," *Washington Post*, January 6, 2017.

16. Matthew Pennington and Jill Colvin, "Trump Says He'd Speak with Kim Jong Un over Nukes," Associated Press, May 17, 2016.

17. Damian Paletta, "China Shrugs Off Trump Twitter Jab on North Korea," *Wall Street Journal*, January 3, 2017.

18. Robert E. Kelly, "The Ultimate Nightmare: Why Invading North Korea Is a Really Bad Idea," *National Interest*, January 30, 2015, www.nationalinterest.org/blog/the-buzz/the-ultimate-nightmare-why -invading-the-north-korea-really-12157.

19. "Why Is the South China Sea Contentious?" BBC News (July 12, 2016), www.bbc.com/news/world-asia-pacific-13748349.

20. Zachary Cohen, "Photos Reveal Growth of Chinese Military Bases in the South China Sea," CNN, May 15, 2016.

21. Idrees Ali, "U.S. to Boost South China Sea Freedom of Navigation Moves, Admiral Says," Reuters, February 27, 2016.

22. Idrees Ali and Matt Spetalnick, "U.S. Warship Challenges China's Claims in South China Sea," Reuters, October 21, 2017.

23. "Transcript: Donald Trump Expounds on His Foreign Policy Views," *New York Times*, March 26, 2016.

24. Helene Cooper, "U.S. Demands Return of Drone Seized by Chinese Warship," *New York Times*, December 16, 2016.

25. Ben Blanchard, "China Lodges Protest After Trump Call with Taiwan President," Reuters, December 3, 2016.

26. Benjamin Haas, "'No Access': Rex Tillerson Sets Collision Course with Beijing in South China Sea," *The Guardian*, January 20, 2017.

27. Damien Van Puyvelde, "Hybrid War—Does It Even Exist?" *NATO Review Magazine*, www.nato.int/docu/review/2015/also-in-2015/hybrid -modern-future-warfare-russia-ukraine/EN/index.htm.

28. Henry Meyer, "Putin's Military Buildup in the Baltic Stokes Invasion Fears," Bloomberg, July 6, 2016.

29. Robin Emmott and Sabine Seibold, "NATO Agrees to Reinforce Eastern Poland, Baltic," Reuters, July 8, 2016.

30. Uwe Klubmann, Matthias Schepp, and Klaus Wiegrefe, "Did the

West Break Its Promise to Moscow?" *Der Spiegel*, November 26, 2009.

31. www.tomdispatch.com/post/176231/tomgram%3A_michael_klare%2C_twenty-first-century_armageddons/.

32. www.theguardian.com/world/2016/un/06/nato-launches-largest-war-game-in eastern-europe-since-cold-war-anaconda-2016.

33. Ryan Browne and Jim Sciutto, "Russian Jets Keep Buzzing U.S. Ships and Planes. What Can the U.S. Do?" CNN, April 19, 2016.

34. Tim Hains, "Trump's Updated ISIS Plan: 'Bomb the Shit Out of Them,' Send in Exxon to Rebuild," Real Clear Politics, November 13, 2015, www.realclearpolitics.com/video/2015/11/13/trumps_updated_isis_plan_bomb_the_shit_out_of_them_send_exxon_in_to_rebuild.html.

35. Adrian Edwards, "Global Forced Displacement Hits Record High," UNHCR (June 20, 2016), www.unhcr.org/en-us/news/latest/2016/6/5763b65a4/global-forced-displacement-hits-record-high.html.

36. Eric Schmitt, "As ISIS Loses Land, It Gains Ground in Overseas Terror," *New York Times* July 3, 2016.

37. "Transcript: Donald Trump Expounds on His Foreign Policy Views," *New York Times*, March 26, 2016.

38. Rick Gladstone, "76 Experts Urge Donald Trump to Keep Iran Deal," *New York Times*, November 14, 2016.

39. Tom McCarthy, "Steve Bannon's Islamophobic Film Script Just One Example of Anti-Muslim Views," *The Guardian*, February 3, 2017.

11. Nuclear Politics—William D. Hartung

1. For a detailed analysis of the genesis and meaning of the Eisenhower speech, see James Ledbetter, *Unwarranted Influence: Dwight D. Eisenhower and the Military Industrial Complex* (Yale University Press: 2011). And for a brief essay by Ledbetter describing the origins of the term see, "James Ledbetter on 50 Years of the Military-Industrial Complex," *New York Times*, January 25, 2011.

2. Transcript of President Dwight D. Eisenhower's farewell address, January 17, 1961, www.ourdocuments.gov/doc.php?flash=true&doc=90&page=transcript.

3. Ibid.

4. On the cost of the Manhattan Project and related efforts involved in building the first U.S. nuclear weapons, see Kevin O'Neill, "Building the Bomb," in Stephen I. Schwartz, editor, *Atomic Audit: The Costs and Consequences of U.S. Nuclear Weapons Since 1940* (Washington, D.C.: The Brookings Institution, 1998), 33–103; Eisenhower's farewell address.

5. Eisenhower's farewell address.

6. On Eisenhower and the bomber decision, see Ledbetter, *Unwarranted Influence*, 100–101.

7. Peter J. Roman, *Eisenhower and the Missile Gap* (Ithaca: Cornell University Press, 1995), 36.

8. Ibid., 132.

9. Christopher Preble, *John F. Kennedy and the Missile Gap* (DeKalb, Illinois: Northern Illinois University Press, 2004), 7.

10. Richard Reeves, "The Missile Gap and Other Broken Promises," *New York Times*, February 10, 2009.

11. On this point see Preble, *John F. Kennedy and the Missile Gap*, 188.

12. "Cover Story: Communism's Collapse Poses a Challenge to America's Military," *U.S. News & World Report*, October 14, 1991, as cited in G. John Ikenberry, ed., *America Unrivaled: The Future of the Balance of Power* (Ithaca: Cornell University Press, 2002), 68.

13. The effort to replace the Soviet threat with regional actors as a justification for high Pentagon spending is discussed in detail in Michael Klare, *Rogue States and Nuclear Outlaws: America's Search for a New Foreign Policy* (New York: Macmillan Press, 1996).

14. For a good synopsis of the statements and activities of the Project for the New American Century, see Tom Barry and Jim Lobe, "Security Strategy Foretold," *Foreign Policy in Focus*, October 2002. For a more detailed look at the role of neoconservatives in shaping the foreign policy of George W. Bush, see John Feffer, editor, *Power Trip: U.S. Unilateralism and Global Strategy After September 11* (New York: Seven Stories Press, 2003).

15. Barry and Lobe, "Security Strategy Foretold."

16. Carl Conetta, "A Reasonable Defense: A Sustainable Approach to Securing the Nation," Project on Defense Alternatives, December 2012, executive summary, 2.

17. For example, in 2014 the Finance, Insurance and Real Estate (FIRE) sector made over $78 million in campaign contributions, more than four times the $17.8 million in contributions made by companies in the defense sector. Data is from the Center for Responsive Politics "Open Secrets" database, www.opensecrets.org/pacs/list.php. The Koch brothers have pledged to spend nearly $1 billion on political groups, right-wing think tanks, and universities in the run-up to the 2016 presidential elections. See Matea Gold, "Koch-Backed Network Plans to Spend Nearly $1 Billion in Run-Up to 2016," *Washington Post*, January 26, 2015.

18. For details on McKeon's links to the defense industry, see William D. Hartung, "Pentagon Contractors and Congress: Defending Special Interests or Promoting the Public Interest," *Huffington Post*, July 17, 2012.

Data on campaign contributions are from the Center for Responsive Politics' "Open Secrets" database.

19. Tim Starks, "Defense Industry Funds Flow to Contenders for Key House Chairmanships," *Roll Call*, July 31, 2014.

20. Data on lobbying expenditures and number of defense industry lobbyists from the Center for Responsive Politics' "Open Secrets" database.

21. Robert H. Phelps, "Ex-Military Men Gain in Industry," *New York Times*, March 23, 1969.

22. Bryan Bender, "From the Pentagon to the Private Sector," *Boston Globe*, December 26, 2010.

23. For more on the activities and political connections of Gaffney and the Center for Security Policy, see William D. Hartung, *How Much Are You Making on the War, Daddy? A Quick and Dirty Guide to War Profiteering in the Bush Administration* (New York: Nation Books, 2003), 53–58.

24. Colin S. Gray and Keith Payne, "Victory Is Possible," *Foreign Policy*, Summer 1980, 14–27. For more on the National Institute for Public Policy and its influence on the George W. Bush administration's Nuclear Posture Review, see William D. Hartung and Jonathan Reingold, "About Face: The Role of the Arms Lobby in the Bush Administration's Radical Reversal of Two Decades of U.S. Nuclear Policy," World Policy Institute, May 2002.

25. For a profile of Loren Thompson and his ties to the defense industry see Jen Dimascio, "Playing Defense—But at a Price?" *Politico*, December 9, 2010. See also Ken Silverstein, "Mad Men: Introducing the Defense Industry's Pay-to-Play Ad Agency," *Harper's Magazine*, April 2010. To his credit, Thompson often discloses his defense industry ties in his own writings, such as his regular column on the *Forbes* website. Robert Pollin and Heidi Garrett-Peltier, "The U.S. Employment Effects of Military and Domestic Spending Priorities: 2011 Update," Political Economy Research Institute (PERI), University of Massachusetts, December 2011.

26. Pollin and Garrett-Peltier, "The U.S. Employment Effects of Military and Domestic Spending Priorities: 2011 Update."

27. For a detailed profile of the companies and locations involved in the production and deployment of nuclear warheads and nuclear delivery vehicles see William D. Hartung, "Bombs Versus Budgets: Inside the Nuclear Weapons Lobby, Arms and Security Project," Center for International Policy, June 2012.

28. Jon B. Wolfsthal, Jeffrey Lewis, and Marc Quint, "The Trillion Dollar Triad: U.S. Strategic Modernization Over the Next Thirty Years," James Martin Center for Nonproliferation Studies, January 2014.

29. Carol Leonnig and Martin Weil, "John Murtha Dies; Longtime

Congressman Was Master of Pork Barrel Politics," *Washington Post*, February 10, 2009; "The Pork King Keeps His Crown," editorial, *New York Times*, January 14, 2008.

30. Raymond Hernandez and David W. Chen, "Gifts to Pet Charities Keep Lawmakers Happy," *New York Times*, October 18, 2008.

31. Frank Bruni, "Donors Flock to University Center Linked to Senate Majority Leader," *New York Times*, May 8, 1999.

32. Lee Fang, "Pentagon Contractors Flock to Mrs. McKeon," *Salon*, February 1, 2012.

33. Dina Rasor, "Not Even a Fig Leaf: The Blatant Self-Dealing of Chairman McKeon," *Truthout*, March 8, 2012.

34. For a detailed description of Lockheed Martin's campaign to save the F-22, see "The Rise and Fall of the Raptor," in William D. Hartung, *Prophets of War: Lockheed Martin and the Making of the Military-Industrial Complex* (New York: Nation Books, 2012), 1–18.

35. Ibid., 12–17.

36. For a good summary of the difference between the Pentagon's budget requests in recent years and what it actually received, see Todd Harrison of the Center for Strategic and Budgetary Assessments, "The FY2016 Budget . . . Here We Go Again," presentation slides for a January 30, 2015, briefing on the FY2016 Pentagon budget. For another view of current Pentagon spending that points out that the Pentagon's base budget is at a historic high in non-inflation-adjusted dollars, see Laicie Heeley, "Fiscal Year 2016 Defense Spending Request Briefing Book," Center for Arms Control and Nonproliferation, February 2015.

37. Ibid.

38. William D. Hartung, "Time to Rein in the Pentagon's Mysterious Slush Fund," *Los Angeles Times*, August 14, 2014.

12. Ignition Points for Global Catastrophe—Richard Broinowski

1. H.L. Mencken, *On Politics: A Carnival of Buncombe* (Baltimore, James Hopkins University Press, 1956).

2. The Atlantic Charter was a joint declaration of war aims released on 14 August 1941 by President Franklin D. Roosevelt and Prime Minister Winston Churchill following a meeting in Newfoundland.

3. Jack Matlock, *Reagan and Gorbachev: How the Cold War Ended* (New York: Random House 2004

4. *Memoirs of Mikhael Gorbachev* (New York: Doubleday, 1996).

5. However, following Russia's annexation of Crimea and intervention in Ukraine in 2014, a majority of Ukrainians agreed with President Petro Poroshenko that Ukraine should join NATO. Strong opposition continued however in the eastern part of the country. At the time of writing, public opinion remains fluid.

6. General Sir Richard Shirreff, *War with Russia: An Urgent Warning from Senior Military Command* (London: Coronet, 2016).

7. Jewish News Service (JNS.org), "In Final Debate, Trump Calls Iran Nuke Deal 'Stupidest Deal of All Time,'" October 20, 2016.

8. Curt Mills, "Trump Calls on China, Iran, to Fix North Korea," *U.S. News*, September 27, 2016.

13. Nuclear Weapons: How Foreign Hotspots Could Test Trump's Finger on the Trigger—Julian Borger

Originally published in *The Guardian* (Julian Borger/Guardian News and Media).

1. www.theguardian.com/world/russia.

2. Carol Morello, "Former nuclear launch officers sign letter: Trump 'should not have his finger on the button,'" Washington Post, October 13, 2016.

3. Peter Huessy, The Prompt Launch Scare, *Real Clear Defense*, November 9, www.realcleardefense.com/articles/2016/11/09/the_prompt _launch_scare_110326.html.

4. www.theguardian.com/world/north-korea.

5. Steven Holland and Emily Flitter, "Exclusive: Trump would talk to North Korea's Kim, wants to renegotiate climate accord," Reuters, May 18, 2016.

6. Gene Gerzhoy and Nick Miller, "Donald Trump thinks more countries should have nuclear weapons. Here's what the research says," *Washington Post*, April 6, 2016.

7. www.theguardian.com/world/iran.

8. www.fas.org/blogs/security/2016/11/trump-disarmer/.

9. www.theguardian.com/us-news/donaldtrump.

10. www.greatagain.gov/policy/defense-national-security.html.

14. The Existential Madness of Putin-Bashing—Robert Parry

1. Matthew Rosenberg, "Joint Chiefs Nominee Warns of Threat of Russian Aggression," *New York Times*, July 9, 2015.

2. Scott Neuman, "Joint Chiefs Nominee Says Russia Could pose 'Existential Threat' to U.S.," NPR, July 9, 2015.

3. Robert Parry, "Ukraine Merges Nazis and Islamists," Consortium-news.com, July 2, 2015, consortiumnews.com/2015/07/07/ukraine-merges-nazis-and-islamists.

4. Robert Parry, "Ukraine Merges Nazis and Islamists," Consortium News, July 7, 2015.

5. Finian Cunningham, "Washington's Cloned Female War-mongers," informationclearinghouse.com, February 9, 2014, www.informationclearinghouse.info/article37599.htm.

6. "Ukraine crisis: Transcript of leaked Nuland-Pyatt call," BBC.com, February 7, 2014.

7. "Interests of the Russian Federation and the United States with regard to Ukraine are incompatible with each other," Коммерсант.ru, December 19, 2014, www.kommersant.ru/doc/2636177.

8. Carl Gershman, "Former Soviet States Stand up to Russia. Will the U.S.?" Washington Post, September 26, 2013.

9. Neuman, "Joint Chiefs Nominee Says Russia Could pose 'Existential Threat' to U.S."

10. Abigail Edge, "New Bellingcat project to investigate cross-border corruption," journalism.co.uk, September 29, 2014, www.journalism.co.uk/news/new-bellingcat-project-to-investigate-cross-border-corruption/s2/a562610.

11. Carmen Russell-Sluchansky, "The Failed Pretext For War: Sey-mour Hersh, Eliot Higgins, MIT Rocket Scientists on Sarin Gas Attack," Mint Press News, April 15, 2014, www.mintpressnews.com/the-failed-pretext-for-war-seymour-hersh-eliot-higgins-mit-professors-on-sarin-gas-attack/188597; Robert Parry, "A Reckless 'Stand-upper' on MH-17," Consortiumnews.com, May 28, 2015, consortiumnews.com/2015/05/28/a-reckless-stand-upper-on-mh-17.

15. Unthinkable? The German Proliferation Debate—Ulrich Kühn

First published in the Carnegie Endowment for International Peace as "The Sudden German Nuke Flirtation," December 8, 2016.

1. "Transcript: Donald Trump Expounds on His Foreign Policy Views," New York Times, March 26, 2016.

2. m.spiegel.de/wirtschaft/soziales/a-1119912.html.

3. Andrea Shalal, "German lawmaker says Europe must consider own nuclear deterrence plan," Reuters, March 16, 2016.

4. www.deutschlandfunk.de/eu-verteidigungspolitik-nach-der-us
-wahl-wir-werden-mehr.694.de.html?dram:article_id=371737.

5. www.faz.net/aktuell/politik/inland/nach-donald-trump-sieg
-deutschland-muss-aussenpolitik-aendern-14547858.html.

6. James Kanter, "E.U. Plans Big Increase in Military Spending," *New York Times*, November 30, 2016,.

7. www.ft.com/content/c4ddcd64-a732-11e6-8b69-02899e8bd9d1.

8. www.bundespraesident.de/SharedDocs/Reden/EN/JoachimGauck
/Reden/2013/131003-Day-of-German-Unity.html.

9. www.ippnw.de/presse/artikel/de/ueberwaeltigendes-votum-fuer
-abzug-u.html.

10. Ibid.

11. www.dw.com/en/new-german-government-to-seek-removal-of-us
-nuclear-weapons/a-4824174.

12. www.new-york-un.diplo.de/contentblob/4847754/Daten/6718448
/160713weibuchEN.pdf; Ben Doherty, "UN votes to start negotiating treaty to ban nuclear weapons," *The Guardian*, October 27, 2016.

13. www.bundesregierung.de/Content/DE/Artikel/2016/09/2016-09
-07-etat-bmvg.html.

14. www.iaea.org/sites/default/files/infcirc549a2-18.pdf.

15. treaties.fco.gov.uk/docs/fullnames/pdf/1991/TS0088%20
(1991)%20CM-1756%201990%201%20OCT,%20NEW%20YO
RK%3B%20TREATY%20ON%20GERMANY%20DECL
ARATION%20SUSPENDING%20OPERATION%20OF%20
QUADRIPARTITE%20RIGHTS%20&%20RESPONSIBILITIES.
pdf.

16. Toby Dalton and Yoon Ho Jin, "Reading into South Korea's Nuclear Debate," Carnegie Endowment for International Peace, March 18, 2013, www.carnegieendowment.org/2013/03/18/reading-into-south-korea
-s-nuclear-debate-pub-51224.

17. Andrea Shalal, "German lawmaker says Europe must consider own nuclear deterrence plan," Reuters, November 16, 2016.

18. "Germany may need own nuclear weapons: Scholz," *Expatica*, January 26, 2006, www.expatica.com/de/news/Germany-may-need-own
-nuclear-weapons-Scholz_135251.html.

16. Law and Morality at the Vienna Conference on the Humanitarian Impact of Nuclear Weapons—Ray Acheson

1. A regularly updated list of endorsing states, along with the text of the Humanitarian Pledge, can be found at www.icanw.org/pledge.

2. Information, documents, and presentations from these conferences can be found at www.reachingcriticalwill.org/disarmament-fora/hinw.

3. Presentations from the fact-based panels can be found online at www.reachingcriticalwill.org/disarmament-fora/hinw/vienna-2014, along with many government statements.

4. Nobou Hayashi, "The fundamental ethical and moral principles for nuclear weapons," ILPI Weapons of Mass Destruction Project, December 8, 2014, http://nwp.ilpi.org/?p=3019.

5. "National statement at the Vienna conference," Decmber 9, 2014, www.reachingcriticalwill.org/images/documents/Disarmament-fora/vienna-2014/9Dec_Ireland.pdf.

6. Hayashi, "The fundamental ethical and moral principles for nuclear weapons."

7. Ibid.

8. Second Conference on the Humanitarian Impact of Nuclear Weapons, chair's summary, Febuary 14, 2014, www.reachingcriticalwill.org/images/documents/Disarmament-fora/nayarit-2014/chairs-summary.pdf.

9. Proposed Nuclear Weapons Convention (NWC), NTI, last updated October 31, 2016, www.nti.org/learn/treaties-and-regimes/proposed-nuclear-weapons-convention-nwc.

10. See the text of the resolution, voting results, and governmental explanations of the vote at www.reachingcriticalwill.org/disarmament-fora/unga/2015/resolutions.

11. For details about the nuclear weapon ban treaty proposed by some civil society actors, see *A Treaty Banning Nuclear Weapons: Developing a Legal Framework for the Prohibition and Elimination of Nuclear Weapons*, Reaching Critical Will, the Women's International League for Peace and Freedom, Article 36, April 2014, www.reachingcriticalwill.org/images/documents/Publications/a-treaty-banning-nuclear-weapons.pdf. For details about the legal gap, see *Filling the Legal Gap: The Prohibition of Nuclear Weapons*, Reaching Critical Will, the Women's International League for Peace and Freedom, Article 36, April 2015, www.reachingcriticalwill.org/images/documents/Publications/filling-the-legal-gap.pdf.

12. See *Ban Nuclear Weapons Now*, International Campaign to Abolish Nuclear Weapons (July 2013), www.icanw.org/wp-content/uploads/2012/08/BanNuclearWeaponsNow.pdf.

13. For details on nuclear weapon modernization programs, see *Assuring Destruction Forever: 2015 Edition*, Reaching Critical Will, the Women's International League for Peace and Freedom April 2015, www.reachingcriticalwill.org/images/documents/Publications/modernization/assuring-destruction-forever-2015.pdf.

14. The report can be found at www.reachingcriticalwill.org/images

/documents/Disarmament-fora/OEWG/2016/Documents/OEWG
-report-final.pdf; For a list of supporters, see www.icanw.org/campaign
-news/support-for-a-conference-in-2017-to-negotiate-a-treaty-banning
-nuclear-weapons.

15. For documents, statements, and reports from the OEWG, see www
.reachingcriticalwill.org/disarmament-fora/oewg/2016.

16. "Building Toward a Nuclear Weapon–Free World," Remarks by
Anita E. Friedt, Astana, Kazakhstan, August 29, 2016, www.state.gov
/t/avc/rls/261327.htm; "US Pressured NATO States to Vote No to a Ban,"
International Campaign to Abolish Nuclear Weapons, November 1, 2016,
www.icanw.org/campaign-news/us-pressures-nato-states-to-vote-no-to
-the-ban-treaty.

17. A New Movement to Ban Nuclear Weapons—Tim Wright

1. "Bringing the era of nuclear weapons to an end," International
Committee of the Red Cross, www.icrc.org/eng/resources/documents
/statement/nuclear-weapons-statement-200410.htm.

2. www.reachingcriticalwill.org/images/documents/Disarmament
-fora/npt/revcon2010/FinalDocument.pdf.

3. www.reachingcriticalwill.org/images/documents/Disarmament
-fora/nayarit-2014/chairs-summary.pdf.

4. www.icanw.org/pledge.

5. www.un.org/sg/statements/index.asp?nid=6557.

6. unoda-web.s3.amazonaws.com/wp-content/uploads/2014/04/HR_
statement_NZ_Wellington_NZIIA.pdf.

7. www.reachingcriticalwill.org/images/documents/Disarmament
-fora/npt/prepcom13/statements/24April_SouthAfrica.pdf.

8. David McNeill, "Nagasaki Mayor attacks Abe for 'betraying' world
over nuclear weapons," *Independent*, August 9, 2013.

9. www.state.gov/r/pa/prs/ps/2014/11/233868.htm.

18. Don't Bank on the Bomb—Susi Snyder

1. Letter from Lockheed Martin, received by Greg Gardner, April 29,
2013.

19. The Heroic Marshall Islanders: Nuclear Zero Lawsuits— David Krieger

1. De Brum, Tony, website of the Nuclear Age Peace Foundation: http:
//www.wagingpeace.org/tony-debrum/.

2. Information on the Marshall Islands' Nuclear Zero Lawsuits can be found at www.nuclearzero.org.

3. "Advisory Opinion of the International Court of Justice on the Legality of the threat or use of nuclear weapons," United Nations General Assembly, A/51/218, 15 October 1996, p. 37.

20. Persistent Violence and Silent Suffering: Marshallese Migrants in Washington State—Holly Barker

1. Paul Farmer, *Pathologies of Power: Health, Human Rights, and the New War on the Poor* (Berkeley, CA: University of California Press, 2003).

2. Census Report, 1958, "Trust Territory of the Pacific Islands," www .pacificweb.org/DOCS/Trust%20TerritoriesPI/1958%20Census%20 tables.pdf.

3. Holly Barker, "Confronting a Trinity of Institutional Barriers: Denial, Cover-up and Secrecy." *Oceania* 85(3)(2015): 376–389.

4. NHPI, "Native Hawaiians and Pacific Islanders in the United States: A Community of Contrasts" (2014), www.advancingjustice-la.org /sites/default/files/A_Community_of_Contrasts_NHPI_US_2014.pdf.

5. Lucky Juda, interview with Carmen Borja at the Burke Museum, Seattle, WA, regarding heath care access in Washington State (2016).

21. Adding Democracy to Nuclear Policy—Kennette Benedict

Originally published in Tom Z. Collina and Geoff Wilson, eds., *Ten Big Nuclear Ideas for the Next President*, Ploughshares Fund, November 2016.

1. William J. Broad and David E. Sanger, "Debate over Trump's Fitness Raises Issue of Checks on Nuclear Power," *New York Times*, August 4, 2016.

2. Elaine Scarry, *Thermonuclear Monarchy: Choosing Between Democracy and Doom* (New York: W.W. Norton & Company, 2014), 39.

3. Craig Lambert, "Nuclear Weapons or Democracy," *Harvard Magazine*, March 2014.

Contributor Biographies

Ray Acheson is the Director of Reaching Critical Will. He is on the board of directors at the Los Alamos Study Group, represents Women's International League for Peace and Freedom on several coalition steering groups, and previously worked with the Institute for Defense and Disarmament Studies.

Bob Alvarez is a senior scholar at the Institute for Policy Studies. He served as senior policy advisor to the Energy Department's secretary and deputy assistant secretary for national security and the environment from 1993 to 1999. Before joining the Energy Department, Alvarez served for five years as a senior investigator for the U.S. Senate Committee on Governmental Affairs. In 1975, Alvarez helped found and directed the Environmental Policy Institute. Alvarez has published articles in *Science*, the *Bulletin of Atomic Scientists*, *Technology Review*, and the *Washington Post*. He has been featured on television programs such as *NOVA* and *60 Minutes*.

Holly Barker is a senior lecturer in sociocultural anthropology at the University of Washington. In her position at the University of Washington, Holly trains Pacific Islander students in research, and remains actively engaged in issues impacting the local Marshallese community. Holly is also the curator for Oceanic and Asian culture at the Burke Museum.

Seth D. Baum is co-Founder (with Tony Barrett) and executive director of the Global Catastrophic Risk Institute and affiliated with the Blue Marble Space Institute of Science, the Institute for Ethics and Emerging Technologies, and the Columbia University Center for Research on Environmental Decisions. He also writes a column for the *Bulletin of the Atomic Scientists*. He lives in New York City.

Kennette Benedict is a senior advisor to the *Bulletin of the Atomic Scientists* and served as executive director and publisher from 2005 until she retired in February 2015. She is a lecturer at the Harris School of Public Policy at the University of Chicago. Previously, Benedict was the director of International Peace and Security at the John D. and Catherine T. MacArthur Foundation.

Julian Borger is *The Guardian*'s world affairs editor. He was previously a correspondent in the United States, the Middle East, Eastern Europe, and the Balkans. He is the author of *The Butcher's Trail*, about the pursuit and capture of the Balkan war criminals.

Richard Broinowski is a former Australian diplomat. He was Ambassador to Vietnam (1983–85), the Republic of Korea (1987–89), and Mexico, the Central American Republic, and Cuba (1994–97). Among his published works are *Fact or Fission: The Truth About Australia's Nuclear Ambitions* and *Fallout from Fukushima*.

Noam Chomsky is the Institute Professor and a professor of linguistics, emeritus, at the Massachusetts Institute of Technology. He is the author of numerous books, including *On Language, On Anarchism*, and a co-author of *The Chomsky-Foucault Debate*, among many other books. He lives in Lexington, Massachusetts.

Lynn Eden is a member of the *Bulletin of the Atomic Scientists'* Science and Security Board and a senior research scholar and associate director for research at Stanford University's Center for International Security and Cooperation. Eden's *Whole World on Fire: Organizations, Knowledge, and Nuclear Weapons Devastation* won the American Sociological Association's 2004 Robert K. Merton award for best book in science and technology studies.

Bruce Gagnon is coordinator of the Global Network Against Weapons and Nuclear Power in Space. His writing has appeared in *Earth Island Journal* and *Le Monde*, and he is the author of the book *Come Together Right Now*. He lives in Maine.

Hugh Gusterson is a professor of anthropology and international affairs at George Washington University, the author of *Nuclear Rites: A Weapons Laboratory at the End of the Cold War* and *People of the Bomb: Portraits of America's Nuclear Complex*, and was a co-editor of *Why America's Top Pundits Are Wrong* and its sequel, *The Insecure American*.

William D. Hartung is the author of *Prophets of War: Lockheed Martin and the Making of the Military-Industrial Complex* and the co-editor, with Miriam Pemberton, of *Lessons from Iraq: Avoiding the Next War*, among other books. Hartung is the former director of the Arms and Security Initiative at the New America Foundation and served for sixteen years as the director of the Arms Trade Resource Center at the World Policy Institute. His articles on security issues have appeared in the *New York Times*, the *Washington Post*, the *Los Angeles Times*, *The Nation*, and *World Policy Journal*.

Michael T. Klare is a professor of peace and world security studies at Hampshire College and the author of *Resource Wars, Blood and Oil,* and *Rising Powers, Shrinking Planet.*

David Krieger is a founder of the Nuclear Age Peace Foundation and has served as president of the Foundation since 1982. He is a member of the Global Council of Abolition 2000 and the chair of the Executive Committee of the International Network of Engineers and Scientists for Global Responsibility.

Hans Kristensen is the director of the Nuclear Information Project with the Federation of American Scientists in Washington, D.C. Kristensen is a co-author of the world nuclear forces overview in the *Stockholm International Peace Research Institute Yearbook* and a frequent advisor to the news media on nuclear weapons policy and operations. He has co-authored "Nuclear Notebook," a regular feature of the *Bulletin of the Atomic Scientists,* since 2001.

Ulrich Kühn is a fellow and a Stanton Nuclear Security Fellow at the Carnegie Endowment for International Peace, and a fellow with the Institute for Peace Research and Security Policy at the University of Hamburg. His articles and commentary have appeared in the *National Interest, War on the Rocks, Strategic Studies Quarterly,* and *Defense One.*

Investigative reporter **Robert Parry** broke many of the Iran-Contra stories for the Associated Press and *Newsweek* in the 1980s. He is the author of *America's Stolen Narrative* and the editor of *Consortium News.*

Theodore A. Postol is professor of science, technology, and national security policy at MIT. In 2001, he received the Norbert Wiener Prize from Computer Professionals for Social Responsibility for uncovering numerous false claims about missile defenses.

Alan Robock is Distinguished Professor in the Department of Environmental Sciences at Rutgers University, New Jersey. He is an International Panel on Climate Change lead author and was a member of the organization when it was awarded the Nobel Peace Prize.

Susi Snyder is the nuclear disarmament program manager for PAX in the Netherlands. She is a steering group member of the International Campaign to Abolish Nuclear Weapons, a Nuclear Free Future Award laureate, and president of the Women's International League for Peace and Freedom, United Nations Office.

Steven Starr is the director of the University of Missouri's Clinical Laboratory Science Program, as well as a senior scientist at the Physicians for Social Responsibility and an associate of the Nuclear Age Peace Foundation. He has worked with the Swiss, Chilean, and Swedish governments in support of their efforts at the United Nations to eliminate thousands of high-alert, launch-ready U.S. and Russian nuclear weapons; he maintains the website Nuclear Darkness.

Max Tegmark is an MIT physics professor who has written over two hundred technical papers and been featured in dozens of science documentaries. He is the author of *Our Mathematical Universe* and his work with the Sloan Digital Sky Survey collaboration on galaxy clustering shared first prize in *Science* magazine's "Breakthrough of the Year: 2003." He is founder (with Anthony Aguirre) of the Foundational Questions Institute.

Tim Wright is Asia-Pacific director of International Campaign to Abolish Nuclear Weapons. He is a member of the international staff team and has been involved in the campaign since 2006.

About the Editor

The world's leading spokesperson for the antinuclear movement, **Dr. Helen Caldicott** is the co-founder of Physicians for Social Responsibility, a nominee for the Nobel Peace Prize, and the 2003 winner of the Lannan Prize for Cultural Freedom. Both the Smithsonian Institute and *Ladies' Home Journal* have named her one of the most influential women of the twentieth century. In 2001 she founded the Nuclear Policy Research Institute, which later became Beyond Nuclear, in Washington, D.C. The author of *The New Nuclear Danger, War in Heaven* (with Craig Eisendrath), *Nuclear Power Is Not the Answer*, and *Loving This Planet* and the editor of *Crisis Without End* (all published by The New Press), she is currently president of the Helen Caldicott Foundation/NuclearFreePlanet.org. She divides her time between Australia and the United States.

Celebrating 25 Years of Independent Publishing

Thank you for reading this book published by The New Press. The New Press is a nonprofit, public interest publisher celebrating its twenty-fifth anniversary in 2017. New Press books and authors play a crucial role in sparking conversations about the key political and social issues of our day.

We hope you enjoyed this book and that you will stay in touch with The New Press. Here are a few ways to stay up to date with our books, events, and the issues we cover:

- Sign up at www.thenewpress.com/subscribe to receive updates on New Press authors and issues and to be notified about local events
- Like us on Facebook: www.facebook.com/newpressbooks
- Follow us on Twitter: www.twitter.com/thenewpress

Please consider buying New Press books for yourself; for friends and family; and to donate to schools, libraries, community centers, prison libraries, and other organizations involved with the issues our authors write about.

The New Press is a 501(c)(3) nonprofit organization. You can also support our work with a tax-deductible gift by visiting www.thenewpress.com/donate.